The Story in the Stars

(Overview of Bible Astronomy:
Mazzaroth in his Seasons)

by
Elder Conrad Jarrell

Dedication

To the Teller of The Story
Who died on a Cross to make it True

All hail,
Desire of all Nations...
All hail!

Cover Illustration:
Photo by By Skatebiker—Own work
https://commons.wikimedia.org/w/index.php?curid=50191314
Thank you, Skatebiker

ISBN 978-1-387-76957-5

© Copyright 2018 by Conrad Owen Jarrell II

Contents

Introduction—The Story in the Stars	1
Chapter 1—Outline of Patriarchal Religion	2
The Gospel in the Heavens	6
A Brief History and Overview of the Zodiac	9
Chapter 2—The Story in the Stars Defended	14
The Origin of Dispensationalism	15
The Defense Continued	16
Chapter 3— More Complete Analysis of the Zodiac	46
The Zodiac Summarized	92
Chapter 4— The Amazing Credibility Gap	96
The Jews	97
The Arabic Peoples	99
The Scientists	107
That Amazing Credibility Gap Thingy	116
Glossary	120
Appendix 1—The Bible Validated	123
Appendix 2—The Constellations Illustrated	129
About The Author	152

Introduction
The Story in the Stars

Archbishop James Usher (1581-1656, 75 yrs) was a scholar and an historian of absolutely first rank. He entered Trinity College at age 13, prepared a detailed Hebrew Chronology in Latin at 15, and received a Master's Degree at 18. At age 19, he debated the Jesuit scholar Henry Fitzsimons and devastated him, with none matching him in debate thereafter. At 20, he was ordained to the Ministry. At 26, he earned his Doctorate, and became Professor of Divinity at Dublin. Ussher was an expert in Semitic Languages and History, his scholarship was described as "miraculous" by contemporary John Selden (1584-1654, 70 yrs; a polymath, English jurist, and scholar in English and Jewish law). Ussher's Hebrew Chronology, the one used in almost all Bibles, remains unexcelled to this day. In 1993, 2005, and 2009, Dr. Floyd Nolan Jones, Th.D., Ph.D., published and revised his *Chronology of the Old Testament*, which I personally consider to be the most authoritative work of its kind extant. Therein Jones confirms, defends, and expands Ussher's chronology, using archaeological finds, astronomical clay tablets, and information not available to Ussher. I steal most all of my Bible dates from Ussher and Jones.

Briefly, Hebrew Chronology...*in Scripture* (Heb. Masoretic text) ...allows the computation of 3418 years from Creation to the Jewish Captivity, which both Ussher and Jones meticulously and precisely date at 586 BC. 586 + 3418 = 4004 BC, the date of Creation. Specifically, Ussher calculates **Creation on Sunday, 6:00 pm, 21 September (Fall equinox) 4004 BC**. From time immemorial (the Jews believe since The Beginning) the Jewish new year began with the first month Tishri, our present Sep-Oct (Moses was later told by God to change the first Jewish month to that of the Exodus, Mar-Apr). Since the Words God spoke to Moses said, "The Evening and the Morning", and it was the time of the equinox, Ussher concluded creation began at 6:00 pm. Since that was undeniably the first day of the first week (and all other weeks since), Ussher said Sunday. It's all right there, in The King James Bible (and its *specific* underlying Hebrew OT text, the Masoretic). It's *missing*, however, from virtually all the modern revised 'bibles' (and their underlying Hebrew and Greek *Roman Catholic* manuscripts).

Gee...I wonder why?

Chapter 1
Outline of Patriarchal Religion

About 6 pm the second Sunday evening of Creation, the eighth day, because of eating the Forbidden Fruit (and the resultant Curse), Adam and Eve were expelled from the Garden (Gen 3:22-24), and turned out into the dark. But, before He cast them out, God had done a simple yet wondrous thing...something Satan had never *imagined*:

> Gen 3:21 Unto Adam also and to his wife did the LORD God make coats of skins, and clothed them.

Their beautiful bodies, created in the image of God, now cursed under Sin, would grow old and bent under the heavy weight of long years, and finally sag to the ground, breathing a last rattling breath. *But God had breathed eternal life into their Spirits and Souls!* So they would fly free at the last, and return to His Arms. Look carefully at *how* we can know, that *God* did this. **First**, *God made coats of skins*. But...whence came those skins? Have you ever been to a slaughter house? I have. The smell of blood and death pervades the thickened air, that resonates with the frightened moans and cries of the beasts awaiting; while one of their fellows is strung up, brained, throat-slit and slowly...*peeled*...before their bulging eyes. *God Himself made coats of skins*, and killed some innocent beast to do it, a beast that had done naught but live as true and innocent as God had made it; then God peeled away its covering, leaving behind a body bloody, dead and naked; then fashioned therefrom skin-coats, fitted to cover other dying naked bodies, into which He intended to breathe new life. **Second**, *God clothed them*. God came to them, and Himself wrapped the warm coats around their cold and dying bodies. Then, He *breathed* into their Spirits and Souls a new kind of life, one they never had before, that would never end a-more...for evermore. Did He kiss them alive anew when He did, as He did afore? My mind doesn't *know*, but my heart *believes* so, and with love everlasting.

> Gen 2:7 And the LORD God formed man of the dust of the ground, and **breathed into his nostrils the breath of life**; and man became a living soul.

> Jer 31:3 The LORD hath appeared of old unto me, saying, Yea, I have loved thee with an **everlasting love**: therefore with lovingkindness have I drawn thee.

These memories, of their first two days, Adam and Eve would carry to their graves. They would form the living core of stories told of yore, to generations new aborning—Creation and Life; Satan, Sin, and Death; and Grace Redeeming. Stories that would be, have been, and will be told, until that Trump shall sound, and Time no more.

As time passed, the Telling of the Tale took form, and grew. The Tale became Told...1) at an Appointed Time, 2) at an Appointed Place, and 3) in an Appointed Way.

> Gen 4:3-4a And **in process of time** [1] it came to pass, that Cain **brought** [2] of the <u>fruit of the ground</u> an offering **unto the LORD** [3]. 4 And Abel, he also brought of the <u>firstlings of his flock and of the fat thereof</u>....

Here we are, with the first two children born to the human race, and they have Religion. But...just as with their parents, in the Garden of Eden...Truth rears its unyielding head. You see, there are *Two Kinds* of Religion: *True* and *False*. True Religion worships God at the appointed *Time*, in the appointed *Place*, and in the appointed *Way*. False Religion is...*different*. False Religion *may* worship God at the appointed *Time*, and even in the appointed *Place*...but ALWAYS *in its own DIFFERENT Way*.

Think about it. Did God clothe Adam and Eve with banana peelings and corn shucks? They themselves at first tried Fig leaves, which is pretty much the same. Think about it some more. When clothing Adam and Eve, did God use a *bloodless* form of life that depended upon human freewill and works to prosper and yield; or did He use an independent, self-roaming *blood-pulsing* form of life, prepared and provided *by God's Free Grace* alone? God will accept True Religion, but He will *NOT* accept *any form* of False Religion. Think about it a lot.

> Gen 4:4b-8 ...**And the LORD had <u>respect</u> unto Abel and to his offering: 5 But unto Cain and to his offering he had not respect**. And **Cain was very wroth**, and his countenance fell.
> 6 And <u>the LORD said unto Cain</u>, Why art thou wroth? and why is thy countenance fallen? 7 **If thou doest well**, shalt thou not be accepted? and **if thou doest not well**, sin lieth at the door. And unto thee shall be his desire, and thou shalt rule over him.

God accepts Abel's Offering—which recalled God's Salvation by Grace, and Redemption by Blood Atonement, *done by God Himself Alone*. God rejects Cain's Offering—which displayed Cain's Pride in *his own* Freewill and Works. Think about it again. Lamb of God... Cumquats of Cain...somehow, it jest don't *synchronize*, do it?

Look what happened. In the Marine Corps, we had a *technical term* for it, but we'll just keep this simple, so little children can understand it: Cain got *Really Ticked-off*. If you add to that, kicking stuff, throwing things, and cussin' real loud, that would come very close to the literal Hebrew: H3966 *me'ôd* + H2734 *chârâh* = properly *vehemence*, that is, (with or without preposition) *vehemently;* by implication *wholly, speedily,* etc. (often with other words as an intensive or superlative; especially when repeated) + to *glow* or grow warm; figuratively (usually) to *blaze* up, of anger, zeal, jealousy [Strong's Hebrew Lexicon]. *Go* ahead, check it out. God even *talked directly* to Cain. *You* can do the same thing today, by just reading *God's exact words*, right out of a King James Bible, to a False Religion Goober (explain how non-Biblical Flap is Demonic Crap). *They* also do the same thing today...they get *very wroth*...and by some, the wroth is **P**iled **h**igh and **D**eep. God's Own Words from God's Own Mouth *did no more good* than God's Own Words from a King James Bible— That, you see, is the dysfunctional nature of the unregenerate mind:

> Gen 4:8 And Cain talked with Abel his brother: and it came to pass, when they were in the field, that **Cain rose up against Abel his brother, and slew him.**

First murder by a human in history. Man kills his own brother. Over a doctrinal difference in Religion. False Religionist kills a True Religionist. The False Religionist is a Heretic, *convicted* by God's Own Words; the True Religionist is Righteous, *obeying* God's Own Words (Abel was also a Prophet, thus he was *precisely* correct—Mtt 23:34-35, Lk 11:49-51). Now, get this straight: THAT IS THE SUM OF ALL RELIGIOUS HISTORY...*WITHOUT ANY EXCEPTIONS*.

> Gen 3:14a-15 And **the LORD God said unto the serpent**, Because thou hast done this, **thou art CURSED**...15 And **I will put ENMITY between thee and the woman, and between <u>thy seed</u> and <u>her seed</u>; <u>it</u> shall bruise thy head, and thou shalt bruise <u>his</u> heel**.

Sadly, none of the other differences really matter, they're just window dressing. *True* or *False*—"Is it IS, or Is it AIN'T?"—that is the *only* difference that ever *really* matters. That is a big chunk of what this little book is all about. You see, what it all comes down to is this:

> GOD *is the Author of all True Religion,*
> SATAN *is the Author of all False Religion, and*
> EACH *False Religion persecutes ALL other religions—*
> THAT *is just the way it is.*

Let's summarize what we have learned about True Religion, so far. At an Appointed Time and at an Appointed Place (both appointed, mostly, by the Patriarch), God's Salvation by Grace was exemplified by the Blood Sacrifice of an innocent animal (appointed by God, no exceptions). Then, the Patriarch (the first was Adam) would Tell the Story—The Coming Seed of the Woman, Who would Redeem His Fellow Seed, Whose Heel would be bruised by the Serpent, and Who would Bruise the Serpent's Head, then Rise to an Eternal Throne, bearing His Fellow Seed with Him.

How do we *know* this Story was Told? Here it is, right out of The Word of God, in the very Words of God, *as God Himself first preached it*, in the gloaming shadows of the Eighth Night:

> Gen 3:14-16, 20-21 And **the LORD God said unto the serpent**, Because thou hast done this, **thou art cursed** above all cattle, and above every beast of the field; upon thy belly shalt thou go, and dust shalt thou eat all the days of thy life: 15 And **I will put enmity between thee and the woman, and between thy seed and her seed**; it shall bruise thy head, and thou shalt bruise his heel.
> 16 Unto the woman he said, I will **greatly multiply** thy sorrow and **thy conception**; in sorrow thou shalt bring forth children; and thy desire shall be to thy husband, and he shall rule over thee....
> 20 And Adam called his wife's name Eve; because **she was the mother of all living. 21 Unto Adam also and to his wife did the LORD God make coats of skins, and clothed them.**

God preached it to Adam the First Patriarch, then Adam preached it to his children, and those Patriarchs among them Called of God (such as Abel) preached it down the bloodline of the Woman's Seed...until the day, 4000 years later, a Jewish Virgin held That Promised Baby in her arms...THEN **HE** *DID IT!*

To summarize, from a sort of overview, think of Patriarchal Religion (an essentially *tribal* religion) as the precursor to the forerunner, Abraham. Abraham would be the mature stage of Patriarchal Religion. Also, by God allowing non-family members into the worship (by conversion *and* circumcision), Abrahamic religion was a *reformation* of Patriarchal Religion into an early form of Public Religion. Finally, God gradually *reformed* Abrahamic Religion into the theological womb, the forerunner, that produced Mosaical Religion—the first complete, overt Public Worship (by conversion *and* circumcision) that God ever instituted in this world.

For a more thorough synopsis of the development of True Religion, see my book, **How to Study The Bible**, Chapter 3, pp. 97-106, *Tent of Abraham, Tabernacle of Moses, Church of Christ* (go internet to "lulu.com", then choose *Shop*, then type *Conrad Jarrell*; also on Amazon).

The fascinating thing we will study next is, *What* God gave to Adam and the Patriarchs *instead of a Bible!*

The Gospel in the Heavens

Just as surely as stones beneath the surface of a rushing stream provide sure footing for the crossing, let us cross over from ignorance to knowledge on these sure passages from Scripture:

> Gen 1:14-15 And God said, Let there be **lights in the firmament of the heaven** to divide the day from the night; and let them be **for signs**, and for seasons, and for days, and years: 15 And let them be for lights in the firmament of the heaven to give light upon the earth: and it was so.
>
> **signs**. H226 *'ôth* (prob. from H225 *'ûth*, A primitive root; properly to *come*, that is, (impliedly) to *assent*); a *signal* (literally or figuratively), as a *flag, beacon, monument, omen, prodigy, evidence*, etc.
>
> Note: It is easy, once told, to see the great Chronograph of the stars, that divides night and day, and allows us to number the days and measure the four seasons and count the years. But, *"for signs"*? For *signals* and *omens* and *prodigies*? Of *What*? Consider the ultimate root meaning—exactly WHO shall COME, and to WHAT will He ASSENT? We shall see. But never forget—*these* are the *exact* words that God spoke, and Moses wrote down, and God did let none of them fall to the ground (1 Sam 3:19).

> Psa 147:4 He [The LORD, v2] **telleth** the number of the stars; **he calleth them all by their names**. (cp. Isa 40:26)
>
> Isa 40:26 Lift up your eyes on high, and behold who hath created these things, that bringeth out their host by number: **he calleth them all by names** by the greatness of his might, for that he is strong in power; **not one faileth**.
>
> Note: "telleth" means "to count", like a bank teller. "Their Names"—God gave the first names to *all* stars that had one, no exceptions; this is of *supreme* importance to note.

> Job 38:31 Canst thou bind the sweet influences of **Pleiades**, or loose the bands of **Orion**? 32 Canst thou bring forth **MAZZAROTH in his season**? or canst thou guide **Arcturus** with his sons? 33 Knowest thou the ordinances

of heaven? canst thou set the dominion thereof in the earth?

> Note: Pleiades, Orion, and Arcturus are various star groups, which are included in the **Mazzaroth** (the 12 major signs of the Zodiac, together with the 36 minor signs associated 3 each with them)—All of them originally named by God, Psm 147:4. "Ordinances of heaven" speaks of the Law of Nature that disposes them, and "dominion" speaks of how the Zodiac has swayed the understanding of men since the Beginning of Time.

Psa 19:1-6 **The heavens declare the glory of God; and the firmament showeth his handywork.** 2 Day unto day uttereth speech, and night unto night showeth knowledge.

3 **There is no speech nor language, where their voice is not heard.** 4 THEIR LINE IS GONE OUT THROUGH ALL THE EARTH, AND THEIR WORDS TO THE END OF THE WORLD. In them hath he set **a tabernacle for the sun**,

5 Which is as a bridegroom coming out of his chamber, and rejoiceth as a strong man to run a race. 6 His going forth is from the end of the heaven, and his circuit unto the ends of it: and there is nothing hid from the heat thereof.

> Note: Psa 19 is much less a metaphor, and much more literal, when the *meaning* of the names of the stars and signs of the Zodiac is taken into account, together with the order of those signs. Then, we have The Story of The Bridegroom, coming to run His Appointed Course, and the Bruising of His Heel as He trods the Serpent's Head. *Much more* in the section following.

Rom 10:17-18 So then faith cometh by hearing, and hearing by the word of God. 18 But I say, Have they not heard? Yes verily, **their sound went into all the earth, and their words unto the ends of the world.**

> Note: Paul by inspiration of the Holy Ghost, quotes Psa 19:4a, thus EQUATING the Story of the Zodiac with the Gospel of Christ—The Bridegroom coming out of His chamber to fetch His Bride.

Rev 12:1-5 And there appeared **a great wonder in heaven**; a woman clothed with the sun, and the moon under her feet, and upon her head a crown of twelve stars: 2 And she being with CHILD cried, travailing in birth, and pained to be delivered.

3 And there appeared **another wonder in heaven**; and behold A GREAT RED DRAGON, having seven heads and ten horns, and seven crowns upon his heads. 4 And his tail drew the third part of the stars of heaven, and did cast

them to the earth: and the dragon stood before the woman which was ready to be delivered, for <u>to devour HER CHILD as soon as it was born</u>.

<u>5 And she brought forth a MAN CHILD, who was to rule all nations with a rod of iron: and HER CHILD was caught up unto God, and to his throne.</u>

> **wonder**. *G4592 sēmeion* (neuter of a presumed derivative of the base of *G4591 sēma* (a *mark;* of uncertain derivation); to *indicate*:—signify); an *indication*, especially ceremonially or supernaturally:—miracle, sign, token, wonder. [Strong's Greek Lexicon]
>
> Note: Ahh, at last we see—by means of those *signs* God put in the heavens—The *Coming* ONE, and WHAT He *assented* to do. When Christ was born in Bethlehem, the sun set thru the sign of Virgo (the Virgin) and the moon rose under her feet (cp. Rev 12:1-2), fulfilling the Promises of those twelve signs of the Zodiac over her head... and sure enough, the Dragon was waiting...

As I said above, so I say once more, "How do we *know* this Story was Told? Here I've shown it, right out of The Word of God, in the very Words of God, *as God Himself first preached it*, in the gloaming shadows of the Eighth Night. God preached it to Adam the First Patriarch, then Adam preached it to his children, and those Patriarchs among them Called of God (and Abel was one) preached it down the bloodline of the Woman's Seed...until the day a Jewish Virgin held That Promised Baby in her arms...THEN **HE** *DID IT!*"

You see, THE BIBLE GOD GAVE ADAM AND THE PATRIARCHS WAS THE GOSPEL WRITTEN IN THE HEAVENS, scribed with stars each *named* by God, and revealed to the Holy Prophet Adam, first of the Patriarchs, most likely starting on the evening of the eighth day (Luke 1:69-70; Act 3:20-21). And so, Adam began to Tell the Story....

> I love to Tell the Story, more wonderful it seems
> Than all the golden fancies of all our golden dreams.
> I love to Tell the Story, it did so much for me;
> And that is just the reason I tell it now to thee.
>
> I love to Tell the Story, 'twill be my theme in Glory
> To Tell the Old Old Story—[The Bridegroom] and His Love.
>
> —Catherine Hankey
(1834-1911, 77 yrs)
[alteration mine COJ]

God first Told the Story, Himself. He created and *named* the groupings of the stars, the Mazzaroth, on the evening of the fourth creation day...*BEFORE* He created the first angel or the first man!

Afterwards, He gave and explained their names to Adam (the first holy prophet) and to him Told the Story of their *Signs*, and thus of all the key events of Time, from Beginning to End. And Adam, the first holy prophet, passed it on to the human race.

A Brief History and Overview of the Zodiac

Re-read Psa 19:1-6 above. IT'S DESCRIBING THE ZODIAC. Observe how Scripture *explains Itself*. Notice *How* The Words of God in The Word of God—each spoken by God to a chosen stenographer, who wrote them each down (and God did let none of His Words fall to the ground, 1 Sam 3:19)—*Tell The Story in the Stars*:

Psa 19:1 The Firmament sheweth **His handiwork**

> Psa 8:3 When I consider thy heavens, **the work of thy fingers**, the moon and the stars, **which thou hast ordained**;

Psa 19:1 The Heavens declare **the glory of God**

> Heb 1:3 [His Son, v1] being **the brightness of his glory**, and **the express image of his person**, and upholding all things by the word of his power, when he had by himself purged our sins, sat down on the right hand of the Majesty on high;
>
> Rev 21:23 And the city had no need of the sun, neither of the moon, to shine in it: for **the glory of God did lighten it**, and **the Lamb is the light thereof**.

Psa 19:1-4 declare...speech...knowledge...voice...line (i.e., "rule, direction")...words...

> Note: There is *Doctrine* (systematic teaching) embedded in that heavenly message—*in the meanings of the WORDS*.

Psa 19:4a Their <u>line</u> is gone out through all the earth, and their <u>words</u> to the end of the world...

> Rom 10:16-18 But they have not all obeyed <u>THE GOSPEL</u>. For Esaias saith, Lord, who hath believed our report? 17 So then faith cometh by hearing, and hearing by the word of God. 18 But I say, <u>Have they not heard?</u> Yes verily, **their <u>sound</u> went into all the earth, and their <u>words</u>** unto the ends of the world.

Psa 19:4b-6 In them hath he set <u>A TABERNACLE FOR THE SUN</u> 5 Which is as <u>A BRIDEGROOM</u> coming out of his chamber, and rejoiceth as a strong man to run a race. 6 His going forth is from the end of the heaven, and **his circuit** unto the ends of it: and there is nothing hid from the heat thereof.

John 3:27-30 <u>John answered and said</u>, A man can receive nothing, except it be given him from heaven. 28 Ye yourselves bear me witness, that <u>I said, I am not the Christ, but that I am sent before him.</u> 29 **He that hath the bride is the bridegroom:** but <u>the friend of the bridegroom</u>, which standeth and heareth him, <u>rejoiceth greatly because of the bridegroom's voice</u>: this my joy therefore is fulfilled. 30 He must increase, but I must decrease.

Matt 25:1,5-6,10b,13 Then shall the kingdom of heaven be likened unto ten virgins, which took their lamps, and **went forth to meet the bridegroom**....5 While the bridegroom tarried, they all slumbered and slept. 6 And at midnight there was a cry made, **Behold, the bridegroom cometh**; go ye out to meet him....10...**the bridegroom came; and they that were ready went in with him to the marriage: and the door was shut**....13 <u>Watch therefore</u>, for ye know neither the day nor the hour wherein **the Son of man cometh**.

Rev 21:2-3,9-10 And I John saw the holy city, new Jerusalem, coming down from God out of heaven, **prepared as a bride adorned for her husband.** 3 And I heard a great voice out of heaven saying, B<small>EHOLD, THE</small> T<small>ABERNACLE OF</small> G<small>OD IS WITH MEN</small>, and he will dwell with them, and they shall be his people, and God himself shall be with them, and be their God....9 And there came unto me one of the seven angels which had the seven vials full of the seven last plagues, and talked with me, saying, Come hither, I will show thee **the bride, the Lamb's wife.** 10 And he carried me away in the spirit to a great and high mountain, and showed me that great city, the holy Jerusalem, descending out of heaven from God,

Rev 19:6-9 <u>And I heard as it were the voice of a great multitude</u>, and as the voice of many waters, and as the voice of mighty thunderings, saying, Alleluia: for **the Lord God omnipotent reigneth.** 7 Let us be glad and rejoice, and give honour to him: for <u>THE MARRIAGE OF THE LAMB IS COME</u>, **and his wife hath made herself ready.** 8 And to her was granted that she should be arrayed in fine linen, clean and white: for the fine linen is the righteousness of saints. 9 And he saith unto me, Write, **Blessed are they which are called unto the marriage**

> **supper of the Lamb.** And he saith unto me, These are the true sayings of God.

This first section explains the difficulty that *Liberal* scholars have always had with Psalm 19—they never could figure out why the 1st part deals with the heavens and the 2d part with the written law. *Grammatical/Literalist* scholars have always seen the Simplicity: *Both* the heavenly message *and* the written message TEACH THE SAME GOSPEL OF JESUS CHRIST. Notice the obvious and *so simple* parallel that sums it all up. Psa 19 tells us that in the heavens, God hath set A TABERNACLE FOR THE SUN, which is likened to a Bridegroom. Rev 19 declares that *when* the Bride comes to the Groom, THE TABERNACLE OF GOD is with men. The immensity of the Gospel, in the tiniest of nutshells! Anyone who seriously attempts to argue with the *historical reality* and the Scriptural *Grammatical/Literalism*, embedded in that *literary figure*, told throughout The Bible, progressively manifests themself as an utter ass. Can I prove that statement? Sure. See Appendix 1—The Bible Validated.

To begin a brief review of the history and archaeology of the Zodiac, it is appropriate to ask 2 Important Questions.

THE FIRST QUESTION: Just what is the Zodiac?

It is how the Ancient People *classified* the stars and their groupings, in the early science of Astronomy. As the Oxford American Dictionary says, in an historical note, "In ancient times, observation of the sun, moon, stars, and planets formed the basis of timekeeping and navigation." Originally, the Zodiac had *nothing* to do with the fortune-telling gimmick called Astrology. Astrology was a form of Satanic dum-dum doo-doo (careful, technical meaning only...we are discussing the science of Astronomy, with overtones of Theology...see Glossary), that arose many years after the Expulsion from Eden, and was wiped out in The Flood:

> Gen 4:26 And to Seth, to him also **there was born a son**; and he called his name <u>Enos</u>: **then** began [H2490 *châlal*] **men to call upon the name of the LORD**.
>
> **began**, H2490 *châlal*. A primitive root; properly to *bore*, that is, (by implication) to *wound*, to *dissolve*; <u>figuratively to *profane* (a person, place or thing)</u>, to *break* (one's word), to *begin* (as if by an opening-wedge).
>
> Hence, "...<u>**Then**</u> **began-profanely** men to call upon the name of the LORD." Men began *properly* on the 8th day.

Shortly after Enos was born <u>in 3769 BC (235 yrs after Creation)</u>, men began to *profane* The Story in The Stars.

profane. Verb, Treat (something sacred) with irreverence or disrespect. Adjective, Relating or devoted to that which is not sacred or biblical; <u>secular rather than religious</u>.
[Oxford American Dictionary]

In other words, men began to *change* The Story in The Stars, from the *religious* purpose that God intended, and told through the Patriarchs, into something...*Different*...something *worldly*, something more to their own liking.

Gee, how do you reckon that happened? I think Satan did it—with those folk pretty much as he did with Eve in the Garden...Lies and Deception ("surely die"... "lest ye die", Gen 3:1-5). After The Flood, Satan squatted and squirted it back into folks' minds again (see 1 Tim 4:1), in conjunction with the Tower of Babel.

For now, let's stick with the science of Astronomy. The Zodiac ("Mazzaroth in his season", Job 38:32) was the ancient classification of stars and their groupings.

Zodiac. An imaginary belt in the heavens extending for about eight degrees on either side of the apparent path of the sun and including the paths of the moon and the principal planets: it is divided into twelve equal parts, or signs, each named for a different constellation. [Webster's New World Dictionary]

ecliptic. A great circle on the celestial sphere representing the sun's apparent path during the year, so called because lunar and solar eclipses can occur only when the moon crosses it.   [Oxford American Dictionary]

For every solar year, there are twelve lunar months. Thus, as the sun *appears* to circle the earth each year (360°), the moon divides that *apparent* path twelve times (30° each). Those lunar divides were called "Houses of the Zodiac." Each house was named for the major constellation dominate therein (Virgo, Libra, Scorpio, Sagittarius, Capricorn, Aquarius, Pisces, Aries, Taurus, Gemini, Cancer, and Leo). Additionally, the houses were grouped into three Books, of four major constellations each. Next, there were three minor constellations in each house, called Decans, which *expanded* the meaning inherent in the major constellation. Finally, there were exceptionally bright stars, in each of these constellations, whose names were *most important* in *clarifying the meaning* of the major and minor constellations. This, in brief, was the Zodiac.

Let's pause here for a little background. Modern astronomers list 88 constellations (of all and assorted sorts). Approximately 40 of these are fairly modern, dating back about 500 years, more or less. Subtract those, and we are left with 48: 12 major and 36 minor, clumped together one with three. Those 48 are the ones that concern us, those (as best we can now tell) are the Mazzaroth, or the Zodiac as we are calling it. For convenience, in *this* book, *these* meanings are the ones we shall use for *those* terms.

THE SECOND QUESTION: Given the Zodiac,
Where does the Story *start*?

There are two *forms* of this question, depending upon whether we're asking about *After* the Flood, or *Before* The Flood.

AFTER THE FLOOD involves a weird creature known as the Sphinx (from Gk. *sphinggo* = "to bind tight or fast; to bind or hold together"), which had the head of a Woman but the body of a Lion. The Sphinx, according to legend, had the annoying habit of meeting lone men travelers, asking them enigmatic questions, and when they couldn't answer, chewing them up and tossing them off a cliff.

That pulls us right into the eternal Man-Woman Question, doesn't it? When the poor slobs can't figure out what the Woman is asking for (and many of them seem unable), they get chewed up and spit out. As tempting as *that* question is, we won't go there. We are discussing Theology and Historical Astronomy, not Heterosexual Harmony.

Back to the point. The *meaning* of the word Sphinx seems to involve the binding, or holding together of something...kinda like *joining* things together. The head (or Beginning) of the Woman, *joined* together with the body (or Ending) of a Lion. And *that* is the Riddle of the Sphinx: Where does the Story of the Zodiac *start*? It starts at the Beginning, with the Woman Virgo; and it Ends with Leo the Lion destroying the Serpent. The Story of the Zodiac tells the story of the FIRST COMING of the Virgin's Seed (in the first third), then it DETAILS His Great Battle at that time (in the second third); and finally tells of His SECOND COMING and Final Triumph (in the last third). In the ancient Zodiac pictured in the Temple of Esnéh in Egypt, a small sphinx is actually placed between the signs of Leo and Virgo. This seems to be the origin of the Riddle of the Sphinx. *After* The Flood, among all the ancient mythologies of the children of Adam, there is One Dominant Theme—A Coming One, of Whom it is said, "He shall bruise thy head, and thou shalt bruise His heel."

If we ask about *BEFORE* THE FLOOD, we get the same Story (see pp. 4-5), beginning with Virgo—The Coming Seed of the Woman, Who would Redeem His Fellow Seed, Whose Heel would be bruised by the Serpent, and Who would Bruise the Serpent's Head; then Come Again, destroy His enemy, and Rise to an Eternal Throne, bearing His Fellow Seed with Him.

Chapter 2
The Story in the Stars Defended

There are three *outstanding* sources for studying the history and archaeology of the Zodiac. First and foremost is the exceptionally thorough and exhaustive research of Frances Rolleston (1781-1864, 83 yrs.), an English linguist and scholar. First published in 1862, it contains a lifetime of her research. It was never finished, so remains only a mass of researched and annotated detail. The edition I have and find quite useful is "MAZZAROTH or, the CONSTELLATIONS and MIZRAIM; OR, ASTRONOMY OF EGYPT", Kindle edition, $2.99. It has a well done Table of Contents, and has been numbered and noted and somewhat organized in a quite helpful manner. Another excellent book, utilizing in part the research of Rolleston, is **The Gospel in the Stars**, by Joseph Augustus Seiss (1823-1904, 81 yrs.), an American Lutheran Minister and Theologian. His book is an exceptionally fine and comprehensive presentation of material. A third excellent book, utilizing Rolleston, is **The Witness of the Stars**, by Ethelbert William Bullinger (1837-1913, 76 yrs.), an Anglican clergyman, Biblical scholar, and Theologian. Both Seiss and Bullinger are excellent, for the most part, on the history of the Zodiac, and the meaning of the names of important elements. And they both provide excellent representations of *the oldest pictures* of the constellations of the Zodiac.

That said, they all sprinkled their work with a few goobers, which the detractors use to justify throwing out the baby with the bath water. I'll do my best to recover the baby, and put on a clean new diaper; then we can watch it kick and laugh. It has quite a story to tell.

A small warning

Both Seiss and Bullinger were *Dispensationalists*, Bullinger actually a hyperdispensationalist (and also a little weird, see Wikipedia). Does that cause us a problem? Not really in the case of Seiss, and only here and there in the case of Bullinger (easy to spot, easy to ignore). Both men are first rate on the *definitions* of words and names in ancient documents, which is why I use and recommend their work. Why is this warning...*worthwhile*? Because...

NOBODY
ON THE KING JAMES BIBLE TRANSLATION COMMITTEE
WAS A DISPENSATIONALIST.

Why?

Because in 1611, nothing like the modern version of dispensationalism had yet been invented. Therefore, *not a word of it* is found in the King James Bible, nor in its underlying Hebrew or Greek texts.

You see, there is this here...*Problem*:

1 Tim 4:1 Now the Spirit speaketh expressly, that **IN THE LATTER TIMES** some shall **depart from the faith**, giving heed to **seducing spirits**, and **doctrines of devils**;

The Origin of Dispensationalism

Satan squatted and squirted into the minds of a Scottish Pastor named Edward Irving (1792-1834) and various members of his congregation. They began getting "revelations", and "visions", and various forms of "spirit writing" during which they jotted down occult stuff that "spirits told them". In 1824, Irving had obtained a copy of a book by a Roman Catholic *Jesuit* Priest named Manuel Lacunza (1731-1801, 70 yrs.), which outlined the first modern form of dispensationalism (*well over 120 yrs AFTER 1611, apparently by expanding* the fantasies of Emperor Constantine's sycophant Lactantius (c. 250- c. 325, ~70 yrs.). **In 1827**, Irving published his own translation of Lacunza under the title, *Coming of Messiah in Glory and Majesty*. Then, Irving wrote about this weird spirit stuff, and what *The Weird Spirits* told him, all during the 1820s.

[I know, *I know*...I'm just telling you the way *They* told it.]

Then, Satan squatted and squirted this stuff into the earholes of a Plymouth Brethren preacher named John Nelson Darby (1800–82, 82 yrs.). He visited Irving's bunch, interviewed them about all the "spirit stuff", went into seclusion for about a year, then came forth spouting and whooping about "Dispensationalism" (*his invented theological word*), thoroughly converted the Plymouth Brethren **in the 1830s**, and travelled all over the world spreading this wonderful "spiritual" revelation. He became known as the father of modern dispensationalism and futurism ("The Rapture"! Again, *his invented theological word*).

Then, **in 1909**, Cyrus Ingerson Scofield (1843- 1921, 78 yrs.)—a devoted Rejoicee of these 'spiritual' wonders of Lacunza the Jesuit, Irving, and Darby—published his famous Scofield Reference Bible... *Dispensationalized* to the core, and *Raptured* into literary glory.

Please note: 1827-1909 is *1,760 to 1,842 years LATER* than 65-67 AD, when Paul wrote 1 Tim 4:1. *Capisce?*

As I said above: "In 1611, nothing like the modern version of dispensationalism had been invented yet. Therefore, not a word of it is found in the King James Bible, nor in its underlying Hebrew or Greek texts." NOT...A...WORD...(which is why Scofield had to stick it all in footnotes—*it's not in the Text*). In the King James Bible, there's only The Word of God in The Words of God (of which God did let none of them fall to the ground, 1 Sam 3:19). True Believers just gotta make do with that little dab, best we can.

Read 1 Tim 4:1, above, one more time. Then...*THINK*: *Jesuit* Priest, "revelations", "visions", "spirit writing", Dispensationalism, Rapture, Scofield Reference Bible...and the *incessant* theme song of virtually all Dispensationalists,

> *My hope is built on nothing less,*
> *Than Scofield's Book and Moody's Press!*

What?...That *JESUIT DEMON STUFF* is *actually* The Word of God in The Words of God? *REALLY?* DANG, People! *Darby* INVENTED the *theological words in the 1830s!* I'm not going to slap you upside the head, like Gibbs does Tony; because to do it right, I'd have to give you a concussion.

Review the historical notes above, and read 1 Tim 4:1 a *third* time (it might help to memorize it). Can you say, "Demon Dum-dum Doo-doo?" *I knew you could!* Now...get up off your knees, read *Brainwashing* and *Dum-dum Doo-doo* in the Glossary, then grab a 1611 King James Bible and run free, right out the door...laughing and laughing and laughing. When you stop to catch your breath, you might want to read my little book, **How to Study The Bible**, Chapter 3, pp. 106-113, *Amillennialism vs.* all *other -isms* (see above). Then, run back here to the Zodiac.

The Defense continued

So, there are three *outstanding* sources for studying the history and archaeology of the Zodiac: Rolleston, Seiss, and Bullinger. But, there are Problems (aren't there always?).

Because her book was never published in finished form, Rolleston's Notes were often hard to come by. Further, she did make her notes available in the early 1800s, when the modern science of Archaeology was just getting underway. Thomas Jefferson is credited with the first scientific digs of some Indian burial mounds in the late 1700s; and the stuff found was so interesting, people started digging into mounds all over the place. Thus, baby archaeology was brought forth kicking and screaming, and it has not quieted down since. Point being, Rolleston's research is based upon *early* searches of published books and papers, not *modern* digs with pick and shovel. As a result, she's in the ball park most of the time, *but* knocks the ball over the fence sometimes, and just plain strikes out a time or two...the curse, you see, that blights all pioneers.

Seiss and Bullinger came along toward the 1880s, after Archaeology was well underway. However, because Rolleston's work was so well done (even given all the pioneer difficulties), they did not do their double-checking as thoroughly as they could have. Result? Some boo-boos, a few of them serious. These oversights have been *compounded* by the majority of professing christians being lured astray by devices of the Jesuits of Rome (and others), in their unceasing war against not only Protestants, but especially against the King James Bible of 1611 and the *majority* of manuscript evidence—which exposes the corruption of the Roman Catholic Manuscripts...especially that of Aleph, B, Alexandrinus, Vaticanus, and Sinaiticus (the most beloved golden idols of the Revised 'bible' editors, *and* the most corrupt).

Beginning in the early 1940s, and greatly accelerating in the 1960s, the majority of professing christians simply tossed the King James Bible and embraced the Revised 'bibles' of the Roman Whore (Rev 17:1-6,9) —which greatly water down, or even remove, the Biblical references to The Story in the Stars. It never occurs to the highly educated idiots (with ignorance **P**iled **h**igh and **D**eep) that reject The Story and the King James Bible, that the problem lies *not so much* with the testosterone might of modern archaeology *as it does* with the Jesuit 'wussy-fied' drivel of their Revised new 'bibles' (and their utterly corrupt underlying manuscript evidence—comprising *less than* 18% of Hebrew texts and *less than* 1% of Greek texts!).

What's the point? This right here:

THE *OVERWHELMING MAJORITY*
of Those who reject The Story in the Stars
ALSO
reject the King James Bible
(and its underlying Hebrew and Greek texts)
and embrace the Roman Whore's new Revised 'bibles'.

As we used to say in the Marine Corps, "It goes with the territory." You might want to keep this in mind...you'll be surprised how often you run into it. Also, here's a helpful new word:

> **apostate.** noun. a person who renounces a religious or political belief or principle. [Oxford American]

> Note: How about renouncing *the entire Bible* (Hebrew, Greek, *and* English); which God inspired, preserved, translated, and did not let a single word fall to the ground? Hmmmm...you reckon *this* verse would apply?

> **1 John 5:10 He that believeth on the Son of God hath the witness in himself: he that believeth not God hath made him a liar; because he believeth not the record that God gave of his Son.**

Just remember one thing: *We will validate The Story in the Stars* (but *not* necessarily any boo-boos by Rolleston, Seiss, and Bullinger—and they did make a few). That said, let's move on.

Some Basic Assumptions of The Story in the Stars

Most detractors of The Story in the Stars like to point out basic assumptions in The Story, and then try to refute them or show them erroneous. Nothing wrong with that, that's a basic approach to refutation. So, let's start with those **BASIC ASSUMPTIONS**...but *validate* each one.

1. *Only* what is recorded in plenary inspired thus inerrant Scripture from God is of ultimate Proof Value (2 Tim 3:15-17)—the presence or absence of opinion among Bible Commentators *may* be of literary and/or historical value, but it is of *zero* Proof Value.
2. The Original Language of Man, down to the Tower of Babel (~ 2242 BC, Ussher & Jones) was Hebrew.
3. For the *builders* of the Tower of Babel, both the Original Language *and* it's Vocabulary were changed, but *some* root forms of *some* Hebrew words remain in almost all languages.
4. God gave the First Names to all stars that have ancient names (Psa 147:4; Isa 40:26).
5. The most important star names will date from more Ancient Times, thus reflecting those God-given Names.
6. The *meaning* of the First Star Names God gave tell a Story of Things to Come (Gen 1:14).
7. Prior to beginning Holy Scripture by Moses, God told the Story of Coming Things to Adam and those patriarchs following by means of those star names.

1. Only Scripture *Proves*, not Commentators

One of the standard whines of King James Bible rejecting detractors of The Story in the Stars is, "It's not found in any of the Commentators." That's because they get their new Revised 'bibles' from Rome, whose Supreme Authority is *not* The Bible, but The Infallible Pope. Therefore, their ultimate authority is *now* Human Opinion, *not* any longer The Word of God in The Words of God. An Infallible Pope surrounded by an army of Ph.D. commentators is a comforting illusion...it makes new Revised 'bible' readers *'Feeeelll Gooooodd'*.

But...God inspired *all* Scripture (2 Tim 3:15-17), choosing both the topics (Isa 8:1) and the words (Jer 36:2,4,17-18), God doesn't let even one of His Words fall to the ground (1 Sam 3:19), the universe will ultimately fail but not one of God's Words will fail (Mk 13:31), and finally God's Scripture—The Word of God in the Words of God—will be the Law Book on the Desk at Judgement Day (Rom 2:16; John 12:48).

Scan back over Chapter 1 and the sections *The Gospel in the Heavens* and *A Brief History and Overview of the Zodiac*. THERE IS THE OUTLINE, IN SCRIPTURE, FOR MOST OF THE MAIN POINTS IN THE STORY IN THE STARS. It is *not* God's fault the Commentators missed it...but it *is* Satan's fault—Proof:

> 1 Tim 4:1 <u>Now the Spirit speaketh expressly</u>, that **IN THE LATTER TIMES** some shall **depart from the faith**, giving heed to **seducing spirits**, and **doctrines of devils**;

Feast on The Word of God in The Words of God...then use King James Bible rejectors' beloved Commentators for toilet paper.

Assumption 1 validated.

2 & 3. ORIGINAL LANGUAGE HEBREW, CONFOUNDED AT BABEL, TRACES OF HEBREW ROOTS REMAIN

The Account of the Tower of Babel is found in Gen 11:1-9. The two passages that provide greatest understanding of these events are

> Gen 9:1 And **God** blessed Noah and his sons, and **said unto them, Be fruitful, and multiply, and <u>replenish the earth.</u>**

> Gen 11:4 And **they said**, Go to, let us build us a city and a tower, whose top may reach unto heaven; and let us make us a name, **<u>lest we be scattered</u> abroad upon the face of the whole earth.**

God told the Human Race when they came off the Ark (they were only 8 of them) to "replenish the earth". After they started breeding and multiplying, most of them decided they wanted to stay in one place and *not* be scattered thru all the earth—the *exact opposite* of what God commanded. What did God do? He Babel-ized their language into over 100 different languages (about the number of families, named and unnamed, according to the table of nations in Gen 10). Then, He scattered them all over the earth *anyway*, just the way He wanted...and it says so *twice*, for emphasis (Gen 11:8-9). So much for that.

Now, let's look at that One Language.

> Gen 11:1 And the whole earth was of **one language** [ie, one single linguistic structure] **and of one speech** [ie, one vocabulary].

Here we get to one of the more serious goobers Rolleston made, and Seiss and Bullinger failed to catch. She *assumed*—"assume" makes an ass of u and me—God 'Babeled' the language *but not the vocabulary*. To save a lot of time and space, God 'Babeled' 'em both. She was trying to figure out how the God-given star names could survive, and she guessed wrong. The names did *not* survive as unchanged words, but some *did* survive as two and three consonant *word roots* in over 100 different languages. Over the next 400 years or so (from ~2242 BC Babel until ~1800 BC Babylon) the human race was not only being scattered, with only the few biggest chunks remaining in touch, but they also had to solve the problem of how to learn and translate and write in over 100 languages, to communicate. It was over 400 years of mass confusion. Around 1800 BC, in new Babylon, some of the pieces started coming together. The details of *that* need not concern us here. Let us simply note that those two and three consonant *word roots* of the original Hebrew, scattered among most languages, made *translating those words back into Hebrew* much easier.

There is a fascinating book entitled **The Word** (2000), by Isaac E. Mozeson, a Hebrew linguist. It was written to argue that one of the greatest contributors to Modern English vocabulary was Hebrew (he notes specifically over 22,000 "coincidences" in etymology); not *only* because of the fascination of early English scholars and their linguistic progenitors with Hebrew Scriptures, but *also* because of that two and three consonant *word root* contribution, by the confusion of tongues at the Tower of Babel, to most languages. *This is exactly what one would expect to find, if all those languages were confounded from One Original Language that was Hebrew!* In the Foreword, Mozeson said,

> Yes, I began from the Biblical given that Hebrew is the Mother Tongue (Genesis, Chap 11). It seems to me that I have begun to prove that "all the earth was of one speech, with a unified vocabulary" (the more words have changed, the more they remained the same)....
>
> With all my idol breaking, I have remained too true to conservative linguistic rules to be iconoclastic. I am grateful for my brief training in linguistics, and for the century of research into Indo-European roots that often made my discoveries possible. I stand on the shoulders of giants, though the linguists wish I would get off their backs.

I will let Mozeson argue his own case, but I strongly suggest you pay close attention.

Rolleston has been roundly ridiculed and even rejected by unbelievers for arguing the antiquity of Hebrew as the ancient tongue of the Zodiac. Now, over a 130 years later, that bold and pioneering woman is being validated. There is, indeed, though not exactly why she surmised, a significant basis for similarities between names and words in other languages and their semblance in Hebrew. As we will see, the ancient Hebrew names and their meanings, found scattered throughout the Zodiac, make for some truly astounding revelations.

So...Rolleston was half-right, but for the wrong reason! There are many traces of the original Hebrew language, residual in some *word roots* in most languages. And, for all practical purposes, that answers many of the detractors' arguments against survival of many of those original Star Names in Hebrew.

Finally, do we have an undeniable proof text for Hebrew being the One Language? No. *But*...we do have a *subtle* but strong argument from Scripture that is irrefutable.

Begin by noticing that Shem and his descendants down to Abraham are mentioned *twice*—once in Gen 10:21-31, and again after the Tower of Babel in Gen 11:10-25. Not only does this double mention focus our attention on Shem and his kids, *but both lists are needed to complete the list of patriarchs down to Abraham.*

Be patient, we're getting there (I told you it was *subtle*).

In the second list, from Gen 11, we find a complete Father to Son lineage from Shem to Abraham. Note that Terah is the father of Abraham. Now, over in the Book of Joshua (*subtle*, see?), we read

> Joshua 24:2-3 And Joshua said unto all the people, Thus saith the LORD God of Israel, **Your fathers** dwelt on the other side of the flood in old time, even **Terah**, the father of **Abraham**, and the father of **Nachor**: and **they served other gods.** 3 And **I took your father Abraham** from the other side of the flood, **and led him** throughout all the land of Canaan, and multiplied his seed, and gave him Isaac.

Here it is—Joshua (inspired of God) is telling the People about "Your Fathers," that is, their ancestors...*but he specifically excludes all except Nachor, Terah, and Abraham*; even though he had Moses' complete record of progenitors back to Shem and Noah. Why? Because he had something important to tell them about *just those three*. What?

That those three started serving other gods...87 years *after* Babel... *until* God took and led *only Father Abraham*.

What's the point? you ask. Oh, good grief...don't make me slap you upside the head like Gibbs does Tony! The *obvious* point is, of all the Patriarchs from Noah and Shem, in the Father-Son line down to Abraham, *only Nachor and Terah served other gods*, and that was *87 years after Babel* (Abraham was recovered by God). The *subtle* point is, by *grammatical/literal* inference, *all of the others back to Shem and Noah faithfully served God!* Use the Kiss Principle: **K**eep **I**t **S**imple, **S**tupid...no *mighta-woulda-coulda*...only and exactly what the precise words God told Moses to write down actually *say*. Of the direct line of Father-Son, from Noah and Shem to Abraham, *only Nachor and Terah served other gods* (exceptions noted)...*and only after Babel*.

Why is that *subtle* point so important? Because, when God 'Babeled' the Tower Builders, that bunch included *EVERYBODY EXCEPT* the Noah-Shem-Abraham Father-Son line (and their immediate families), *who kept obeying God*. And *that* means the Noah-Shem-Abraham Father-Son line (and their immediate families) were *not* Babeled, but CONTINUED TO SPEAK THE ONE LANGUAGE AND VOCABULARY! And what was that? HEBREW! How do we know? Because their lineal blood-descendant from Abraham, Moses (430 years later), was still speaking and writing in Abraham's language—AND IT WAS HEBREW!

This proof does not *say* the original language was Hebrew; but grammatically, literally, and logically it undeniably *infers* it. Why is this argument so strong? *The only way to refute this proof* is, at some point, *to deny a plain statement of Scripture*. That has consequences,

> 1 John 5:10 He that believeth on the Son of God hath the witness in himself: **he that believeth not God hath made him a liar**; because he believeth not the record that God gave of his Son.

Assumptions 2 & 3 validated.

4. GOD NAMED THE STARS

> Psa 147:4 He telleth the number of the stars; **he calleth them all by their names**.

> Isa 40:26 Lift up your eyes on high, and behold who hath created these things, that bringeth out **their host** [the heavens v22, hence stars] by number: **he calleth them all by names** by the greatness of his might, for that he is strong in power; **not one faileth**.

That settles *that*, doesn't it?

One more thing...notice "not one faileth". One of the huge arguments of the detractors of The Story in the Stars is to argue that Rolleston was wrong about Hebrew (we've settled that), and that she (also Seiss and Bullinger) scrabbled around and made up some star names from residual evidence that didn't actually *say* it. Well, God said about the stars and their names, "Not one faileth". Doesn't that *imply*, that in the broken and residual pieces of star names left over from Babel, that one should be able to fit *some* of those pieces back together into those star names? Sure looks like it to me.

Assumption 4 validated.

5. SOME STAR NAMES FROM ANCIENT TIMES REFLECT GOD-GIVEN NAMES

Having shown that the Original Language was Hebrew, thus that all those original Ancient Star Names *must* have been in Hebrew, then one would expect to find *repeatedly* that the oldest star names in the Zodiac would be in Hebrew. And that is *exactly* what is found in the ancient records. I will show this over and over from Rolleston, Seiss, and Bullinger's work outlined in Chapter 3.

Assumption 5 validated.

6 & 7. THE *MEANING* OF THE FIRST STAR NAMES GOD GAVE TELL A STORY OF THINGS TO COME (GEN 1:14), AND GOD TOLD THAT STORY TO MEN.

Gen 1:14 And God said, Let there be lights in the firmament of the heaven to divide the day from the night; and **let them be for SIGNS** ['ÒTH H226], and for seasons, and for days, and years:

It should come as no surprise that the stars and their positions have been used to time days, seasons of the year, and the years themselves by all civilized peoples from the dawn of...well, *Time*. Our clocks are set by reference to several master clocks which themselves, for decades now, have been precisely set by continual electronic reference to star positions. But, that's not the Whammy.

The Whammy is, the meaning of the Hebrew word *'ôth*, translated "signs" in v14.

> **'ôth** H226. Probably from H225 (in the sense of appearing); a signal (literally or figuratively), as a flag, beacon, monument, **omen, prodigy,** evidence, etc.
>
> **'ûth** H225. A primitive root; properly **to come**, that is, (impliedly) **to assent**.

The meaning of this Hebrew word is pregnant with portent. First, look at *omen*, it means a portent of good or evil—a *portent* being "a sign or warning that something, especially something momentous or calamitous, is likely to happen." [Oxford American] Now consider *prodigy*—"a person, especially a young one, endowed with exceptional qualities or abilities." [Oxford American] Finally, consider the root meaning: to come, that is, to assent. Now, let's put all this together:

> A Person, endowed with exceptional qualities and abilities, is going To Come and will Assent to something momentous.

How about

> Gen 3:15 [God speaking to the Serpent, v14] And I will put enmity between thee and the woman, and between thy seed and **her seed**; <u>it</u> **shall bruise thy head, and thou shalt bruise <u>his</u> heel.**

A Person Who turns out to have two natures, God and Man (*exceptional* enough?), Who gets His heel bruised by dying on a Cross for over a billion people and redeeming them from sin (to which He *assented* in covenant), Who is resurrected three days later (*momentous* enough?), Who ascends to Heaven and is crowned King (he certainly has *quality*), and Who promises to Return a Second Time, destroy that Serpent in Hellfire (would that *bruise his head*?), and then take the Redeemed to Glory (*able* enough?).

What's my point? You would be surprised how many detractors of The Story in the Stars *admit* that God named all the stars, and will even quote the same verses I did to prove it, and then take the butt dumb position that *God never told anybody those Star Names!* Then use *That* idiocy for a reason to *deny* there ever was *any* Story in the Stars.

<u>First</u>, note the complex definition of the Hebrew word *'ôth*; <u>Second</u>, observe the Promise in Gen 3:15; and <u>Third</u>, read my extended proof that all the *essential points* in The Story in the Stars are repeated throughout the Old and New Testaments, from Genesis to Revelation (see the entirety of Chapter 1)—I decided to start this whole book this way, with that chapter, in order to answer this *dum-dum doo-doo* argument in detail BEFORE *I even got to it!* Check the meaning of that technical term in the Glossary, we are studying Historical Theology and Prophecy and we need *precision*—**these three points establish** beyond confutation that the Star Names not only tell The Story, but then *God told That Story* to the entire human race thru a line of 20 Patriarchs (from Adam to Noah to Abraham), pointing to the stars instead of Bible verses, for 2513 years *before* He told Moses to write the first word of inspired Scripture.

Here is the tombstone for this butt dumb twaddle:

> Amos 3:7 **Surely** the Lord GOD will do **nothing**, but he **revealeth** his secret unto his servants the **PROPHETS**.

Adam, Able, and other pre-Flood patriarchs *were Prophets.*

Assumptions 6 & 7 validated.

So...How do the detractors complain about these Assumptions? They whine,

> "Note that all...assumptions must be true for the gospel in the stars theory to be true. None of these assumptions can be proven, so they truly are assumptions. If any of the...assumptions are not true, then gospel in the stars is not true." [my emphases, COJ]

[I'm going to be nice, and not cite the author's name]

Based on the evidence I have tendered up to this point, I will rejoin with just one word: POOH.

I am going to refer to this detractor a lot. Why? He makes some of the *best* arguments against The Story in The Stars. As my high school speech instructor taught us, in debate class, "If you can refute the best, you can laugh at the rest." He is one of the science writers for *Answers in Genesis*. He is a good researcher. I have read some of his other stuff and like it. Because I like his work, and respect both him and *Answers in Genesis*, I choose not to cite his name. No need to make this personal. It isn't. It's factual.

Having validated the 7 Basic Assumptions *necessary* to The Story in the Stars, we will continue on, more or less randomly; and deal with **a number of other objections** proffered by the detractors.

ROLLESTON'S SUPPOSITIONS ABOUT THE 12 SIGNS OF THE ZODIAC AND THE 12 TRIBES OF ISRAEL

Rolleston argued circuitously, and with no hard evidence, that each of the 12 Tribes had one of the 12 Zodiacal major signs. Seiss and Bullinger, sadly, took much the same tack. Apparently, they were trying to offer some kind of zodiacal justification involving Gen 49:9 "Judah is a lion's whelp..." The problem is, Rolleston, Seiss, and Bullinger's approach is fallacious and bungled. It does not matter one whit whether the 12 Tribes each had a zodiacal sign or not. *Is Judah related to Jesus?* Oh, yes, he's a direct lineal ancestor (Matt 1:1-16; Luke 3:23-34). These two passages, together with Gen 49:9-10 and Rev 5:5,9 and 22:16, are all that are needed to identify Jesus, The Lion of the Tribe of Judah, with Leo the Lion, who is trampling on the head of the Serpent! Assumption 1, we prove from Scripture.

Gen 49:9 **Judah is a lion's whelp**: from the prey, my son, thou art gone up: he stooped down, he couched as a lion, and as an old lion; who shall rouse him up? 10 **The sceptre shall not depart from Judah, nor a lawgiver from between his feet, until <u>Shiloh</u> come; and unto him shall <u>the gathering of the people</u> be**.

—taken together with—

Rev 5:5 And one of the elders saith unto me, Weep not: behold, **the Lion of the tribe of Juda, the Root of David**, hath prevailed to open the book, and to loose the seven seals thereof....9 And they sung a new song, saying, <u>Thou art worthy to take the book, and to open the seals thereof</u>: for **thou wast slain, and hast redeemed us to God by thy blood out of every kindred, and tongue, and people, and nation**;

—and with—

Rev 22:16 I JESUS have sent mine angel to testify unto you these things in the churches. **I am the root and the offspring of David, and** THE BRIGHT AND MORNING STAR.

Furthermore, when Jesus walked into Heaven in Rev 5, He was then crowned with Glory and Honor; and now wields the Sceptre, seated by His Father's side (Rev 3:21).

Rolleston, Seiss, and Bullinger argued *wrongly*...but they were *right* anyway...*because*...those Stars *do* tell a Story—*if* you look at them with a King James Bible. Point made.

ROLLESTON'S USE OF THE WORD "DECAN"

As we shall see in the next chapter, Rolleston arranged the 48 ancient constellations into the 12 major zodiacal signs, each with 3 minors *she chose to call "Decans"*. The ancient folk divided the 12 signs into decans because: the 12 signs are arranged in a circle, following the annual path of the sun, thus dividing the ancient 360 day circle (360°) into 30 days (30°) for each major sign—resulting in each 30 days being divided into 3 sections for the minor signs, each sign thus having a 'decade' of 10 days (10°); and this seems to be the conceptual origin for the term "decan".

The problem is, it's just not that simple in the ancient records. In those old cultures, they often had different signs ruling different decans. These different ancient cultures, though using many of the same words (such as "signs" and "decans") seem to get 'em all scrabbled up and mixed around. Please forgive me, but it seems to me that way back in some ancient time, they all got Confounded into a Babble. My Goodness! How do you suppose *that* happened?

Rolleston bases her attempt to clarify upon Ptolemy's list of 48 ancient constellations—12 major, each with 3 minor—but she also seems to rearrange things a bit, *based upon the oldest discernible names of the brightest stars*, and their relationships in this 360 day (360°) sun circuit through the sky. She says in one place,

> ...The three decans attributed to each sign come to the meridian with it... (Notes 1865 ed., part 5, p. 15)

Also it seems, based on this sketchy evidence, *she chose to use the ancient word "decan"* (used *variously* by the ancients) *to mean each 10 days associated with a minor sign*, thus bringing a measure of order out of a Babel-ized confoundation. *In most cases*, she seems guided by the most ancient star names she could find, tending to rely on the most ancient of those, the Hebrew names.

The detractors jump on her use of Decan. Oh, they admit the antiquity of the word, as well as the jumble of evidence I gave you in the previous paragraphs, but they condemn Rolleston *for deciding to use Decan so precisely*, to describe the 10 day division they all admit exists. Instead of Decan, what if she had chosen to use "Doojigger" or "Doohickey"? Would that have made any *logical* or *arrangement* difference? Certainly not. At least her choice of the word Decan is historical, and is logically connected with the sun circuit (the meaning of the word *is* based on "ten"). The detractors are simply looking for some means to discredit her. Here is what one of them says,

> ...It is a mystery as to where her arrangement of these decans came from. Given the generally poor manner that Rolleston handled sources and her ability to create false history, I conclude that Rolleston probably misunderstood...and that she essentially created her arrangement of the decans herself....
> **Please note that my attempt to explain how Rolleston established her system of decans is conjecture.** I cannot find a precedent for her decans in the literature, and this arrangement appears to be unique in the gospel in the stars, suggesting that this arrangement originated with Rolleston.
> [Again, I respectfully decline to name. My emphases, COJ]

IF there were a Tower of Babel, and IF there were a Confoundation of Language (with one being multiplied into over 100), and IF there were over 400 following years of scattering confusion, and IF there were a Story in the Stars so confounded, and IF that original language was Hebrew and the confounding left many two and three consonant *word roots* in most of those new languages, and **IF** faithful adherents of that one language were left linguistically untouched, and **IF** God inspired men of that original language to write those historical facts in a Book of Scripture, and **IF** God included plot lines and key points of That Story in the Stars *in that Book of Scripture*... **THEN**...the broken fragments of That Story would lie among the shards of that linguistic confoundation, **AND** there would be tell-tale clues in the Hebrew two and three consonant *word roots* in those broken fragments of star names, **AND** That Inspired Book of Scripture (and none other!) would be the greatest clue and the surest glue with which to reassemble those broken fragments of star names back into The Story in the Stars.

Based upon events and facts and Scriptures given, in my present retelling of the Story in the Stars, and following Rolleston's lead (but for some *different* reasons), *I ALSO CHOOSE TO USE THE ANCIENT TERM DECAN* for those ten day divisions given to each minor constellation. If anyone else decides to shout, "Poo-bah! I'm a-gonna use "Doohickey" and "Doojigger"!"...well then, go right ahead.

ROLLESTON'S INTERPRETATION OF ORION

This is one of the areas where the best you can say for Rolleston, Seiss, and Bullinger's reasoning is, *"Goober."* Sadly, they bungled it... and the detractors gleefully thump their heads.

I am not writing this book to defend Rolleston, Seiss, and Bullinger. I'm writing it to tell The Story in the Stars. So, I take a different tack, to prove Orion *definitely is* a type of Christ.

The name of Orion is found 3 times in Scripture (Job 9:9 and 38:31, both mentioned with Mazzaroth, and Amos 5:8). Rolleston was right to point out the Hebrew word is *kesîyl*:

> **kesîyl** H3685. The same as H3684 ; any notable *constellation*; specifically *Orion* (as if a *burly* one). [Strong's Heb lexicon]

> **kesîyl** H3684. *FOOL, stupid* fellow, *dullard, simpleton, arrogant* one. [Brown, Driver, Briggs Heb lexicon, my emphasis COJ]

But, she and the others *wrongly defined* it. The primary Hebrew meaning of Orion is The Fool. It seems they *all* missed the theological implications of Substitutionary Atonement. Even the detractors missed this important point:

> ...For instance, the eight times that the word *fool* appears in Proverbs 26, this [*kesîyl*, COJ] is the word used. Thus,

by the Hebrew name for him, we can see that Orion is not an individual worthy of respect and devotion. To equate this fool with a type of Christ at the very least seriously borders on blasphemy, and most Christians ought to find this offensive. [Again, I respectfully decline to name.]

I emphasize again, they *all* missed the theological implications of Substitutionary Atonement.

> Isa 53:4-6 **Surely he hath borne our griefs, and carried our sorrows**: yet we did esteem him stricken, smitten of God, and afflicted. 5 But <u>he was wounded for our transgressions, he was bruised for our iniquities: the chastisement of our peace was upon him; and with his stripes we are healed.</u> 6 All we like sheep have gone astray; we have turned every one to his own way; and **the LORD hath laid on him the iniquity of us all.**

Permit me to illustrate. I once was preaching in a church fellowship meeting in Georgia. I was dealing with the subject of Substitutionary Atonement, teaching that Christ took the place of the Elect in the Judgement and Wrath of God, and that *all of their sins were placed upon Him*, and that He died for those sins; thus making *Atonement* for those for whom He died, as their *Substitute*. I cited a number of verses like these, *that explicitly say the sins of God's People were all laid upon Him:*

> Heb 9:28 So **Christ was once offered to bear the sins of many;** and unto them that look for him shall he appear the second time without sin unto salvation.

> 1 Pet 2:24 **Who his own self bare our sins in his own body on the tree**, that we, being dead to sins, should live unto righteousness: <u>by whose stripes ye were healed.</u>

> 1 John 2:2 **And he is the propitiation for our sins: and not for ours only, but** <u>also for the sins of the whole world</u>.

I then pointed out the undeniable conclusion that Christ—though He never *committed* a single sin in His entire lifetime—thus became *The Most Sin-full Man That Ever Lived*...each of us bears *only* our own sins, but Christ bore the sins *of the whole world*.

At that point, an ordained idiot (yes, some idiots do get ordained) jumped up and shouted, "Heresy! Heresy! Christ was not sinful!" At least half a dozen other ministers pulled him back to the pew, explaining to him that *I was theologically correct*. That idiot never liked me after that, and I lost my respect for him (how do you respect an idiot who rejects Bible verses *that say it?*).

What is my point? Substitutionary Atonement means Christ bore, and died for, *every single sin...of every single one...of His People*. AND THAT INCLUDES THE SIN OF FOOLISHNESS.

> Psa 14:1-3 **The FOOL hath said in his heart, There is no God**. They are corrupt, they have done abominable works, there is none that doeth good. 2 **The LORD looked down from heaven upon the children of men, to see if there were any that did understand, and seek God. 3 They are all gone aside, they are all together become filthy: there is none that doeth good, no, not one**.

> Pro 24:7-9 **Wisdom is too high for a FOOL**: he openeth not his mouth in the gate. 8 He that deviseth to do evil shall be called a mischievous person. 9 THE THOUGHT OF **FOOLISHNESS** IS SIN: and the scorner is an abomination to men.

> Rom 1:18,21-22 For the wrath of God is revealed from heaven against all ungodliness and unrighteousness of men, who hold the truth in unrighteousness...21 Because that, when they knew God, they glorified him not as God, neither were thankful; but became vain in their imaginations, and **their FOOLISH heart was darkened. 22 Professing themselves to be wise,** THEY BECAME **FOOLS**...

Remember *how* Jesus became The Most Sin-full Man That Ever Lived? Just so, by Substitutionary Atonement, *Jesus became The Greatest Fool That Ever Lived*. Psa 14 teaches that the entire human race are Fools, Pro 24 teaches the thought of Foolishness is sin, and as we know Jesus bore the sins of *the whole world*.

Thus, it is quite reasonable to view the constellation of Orion the Fool as being a type of Christ as The Sin-bearer—bruised in the heel by the Enemy, as he bruises the Enemy's head (Gen 3:15).

This is an excellent example of how the Names God gave the Stars, along with the survival of those ancient Hebrew names, can help us know and tell and reconstruct, from Babeled confusion, that wonderful Story in the Stars.

Rolleston's arrangement of Constellations

Of the 48 constellations listed by Ptolemy, Rolleston along with Seiss and Bullinger replaced three of them with three others (all composed of pieces of those Ptolemaic constellations and their brightest star names). These replacement constellations are The Band (binding the two fishes in Pisces together), The Southern Cross, and Coma (found within the newer constellation called Berenice's Hair). Let's discuss them one at a time.

The Band

> One of the detractors I've been quoting frequently has this to say:
>
>> One of the three additions is the bands tying the fish together in Pisces. Rolleston *claimed* to have found an ancient source that separated the fish and the bindings into two separate constellations, so *apparently* she decided that this was a primordial constellation, *though she gave no reason for this.*
>
> [Again, I respectfully decline to name. My emphases, COJ]

Then, having manufactured this *apparent* rebuttal, he simply moves on and doesn't mention it again. This detractor is laboring against a *cognitively dissonant* barrier that will not let him acknowledge even the possibility of his misunderstanding. Remember above, while validating the *Assumptions* underlying The Story in The Stars, I quoted his denial of the truth of *any* of them, and his consequent conclusion that therefore The Story was *entirely* false? Well, here we are, bumping into it again. Let me point out 3 things his *cognitive dissonance* is oblivious to...*though right in front of his eyes.* 1st—In his own words, "Rolleston claimed to have found an ancient source that separated the fish and the bindings into two separate constellations." 2nd—Again in his own words, "So apparently she decided that this was a primordial constellation." If YOU had found such an ancient source, separating such constellations that had easily predated Ptolemy by over a thousand years...*what would YOU "decide"?* 3rd—Once more in his own words, "She gave no reason for this." Forgive me for being so painfully obvious, but she did. *Her reason was the very first thing I just pointed out that she claimed—the ancient source!* She simply put the pieces back together. I think the best thing for us to do is what the detractor did—just move on, and not mention something so embarrassingly obvious again.

The Southern Cross (Crux).

First, let's confirm a fact—IT WAS LAST SEEN IN THE HORIZON OF JERUSALEM *ABOUT THE TIME CHRIST WAS CRUCIFIED*, and it most assuredly passed beneath the horizon due to procession of the equinoxes. Our favorite detractor says,

> In Ptolemy, the stars that comprise Crux were part of Centaurus, and *descriptions of it as anything else are rare. Certainly, any descriptions of it as a cross is modern*, despite what supporters of the gospel in the stars claim.
>
> [Again, I respectfully decline to name. My emphases, COJ]

Two quick questions come to mind. 1st—Even *rare* descriptions *does* mean alternate descriptions were *There*...right? Even more importantly, they were not a part of Centaurus. 2nd—Differing ancient descriptions, of *Something* not of Centaurus...doesn't that *imply* a period of *Confusion*, way back yonder in the Olden Time?...maybe something *Babeled*? Be honest, Detractor; can you assure us..."*Certainly*"...that nothing such *ever* happened? We will leave that one right there also, just as the detractor did.

Coma

The constellation called Coma Berenice represents the hair of Queen Berenice II of Alexandria. She died in 221 BC, and the constellation name began appearing about a century later. The constellation does not have any particularly bright stars, rather appears as a cluster of faint stars easily seen on a clear night. Ptolemy mentioned this faint cluster, but did not include it in his grouping of 48. Seiss and Bullinger, appealing to the Dendera planisphere, describe the picture of a Woman holding a small Child. Seiss wrote,

> The Greeks knew not how to translate it, and hence took *Coma* in the sense of their own language, and called it *hair —Berenice's Hair*.   [Seiss, 1882, p.29]

Bullinger shared a similar reasoning with Seiss. Both of them shared a similar opinion with Rolleston, though she argued somewhat differently. You see, the word *Coma* in the Dendera planisphere comes most probably from the Heb. word *kamahh* H3642, to long for. Bullinger related it to the Heb. word *chemdah*, to desire. There is one other very strong point to make—the *antiquity* of the pictures in the Dendera planisphere. The physical building, thus the pictures on the ceiling, was constructed most likely in the 1st century BC. Some detractors argue fallaciously that the zodiac pictured is no older than that. Of course, that is as foolish as arguing that a picture painted in 2018 AD of Alexander the Great proves he could not have existed in 330 BC. Arguments for the actual antiquity of the planisphere reach as far back as to the Egyptian New Kingdom. Others, arguing from the style of the pictures, claim similarities to Mesopotamian zodiacs dating back to around 2000 BC. Let us just agree that the *historical antiquity* of the planisphere is much older than 1st century BC, when it was *physically* reproduced in Dendera. Way back Yonder, somebody used the cluster of faint stars to picture a Woman holding a little Baby, and named it *Coma*, The Desired One...and it was *not* a part of Centaurus. Rolleston believed and argued that this picture referred to the constellation Virgo, where a Virgin is pictured holding a sheaf or branch of grain (most believers in The Story in The Stars believe this to be a picture of Gen 3:15 and the Seed of the Woman). The Seed of the Woman in Gen 3:15 is obviously a Child. Furthermore, the Heb. word *seed* literally means "semen virile"—*Her* semen! Women do not produce semen, they make eggs—this is the most beautiful and concise picture of the Virgin Birth in the entire Bible. Rolleston believed that *Coma* was a literal picturing of *Virgo* with the metaphorical Seed in her hand. Our oft-quoted detractor has this to say of Rolleston's explanation, even admitting its plausibility:

> Rolleston...thought that Coma represented the branch or sheaf of grain that Virgo is normally depicted as holding. **One could get that understanding from the Dendera planisphere**, for the scale is difficult to interpret, and the fuzzy appearance of the Coma star cluster could be said to resemble a sheaf of grain. <u>Incidentally, Rolleston consistently refers to the sheaf as a branch, in an obvious connection to Isaiah 11:1.</u> However, **that branch is from a stump of a tree**, <u>and Virgo always is depicted with a sheaf of grain, not a tree branch.</u>
>
> [Again, I respectfully decline to name. My emphases, COJ]

Isa 11:1 And there shall come forth a rod out of the stem of Jesse, and a **Branch** [*nêtser* H5342] shall grow out of his roots:

> **Branch** *nêtser* H5342. Strong: In the sense of *greenness* as a striking color; a *shoot*; figuratively, a *descendant*. Brown-Driver-Briggs: *Sprout, shoot, branch* (<u>always figuratively</u>). [My emphases, COJ]

Two points. 1st—When translated *Branch*, *nêtser* is always figurative. 2nd—*nêtser* NEVER means a tree stump. Are you beginning to appreciate why I am not overly impressed by this guy's *opinions* about The Story in The Stars?

Rolleston in her notes has a fascinating quote from a Muslim writer named Albumasar (787-886, 98 yrs), about Dendera:

> There arises in the First Decan, as the Persians, Chaldeans, and the Egyptians, the two Hermes and Ascalius teach, a young woman, whose Persian name translated into Arabic is <u>Adrenedefa</u> [COJ, note the components: Adre-**nedefa**], a pure and immaculate virgin, holding in the hand two ears of corn, sitting on a throne, nourishing an infant, in the act

of feeding him, who has a Hebrew name (the boy, I say), by some nations named *Ihesu*, with the signification *Ieza*, which in Greek call Christ.

Rollestan said she thought the word *Ieza* was the Heb. word *yesha*, which means "to save". Obviously references to the name Jesus. Sadly, we can't find the quote! The only specific book by Albumasar she mentioned was *The Book of Flowers*...the quote is not in that work. It's goobers like this that reading Rolleston's unfinished Notes sometimes make you want to throw your iPad across the room and scream. Rolleston comments on the name *Adre**nedefa***, arguing it is based on the Hebrew word *nedâbâh* H5071 and means, "a pure virgin, offering"; and cites as evidence,

> Exo 35:29 The children of Israel brought **a willing offering** [*nedâbâh* H5071] unto the LORD, <u>every man and woman</u>, whose heart made them willing to bring <u>for all manner of work,</u> which the LORD had commanded to be made by the hand of Moses.

Rolleston stretches a bit, saying this means "a pure virgin, offering". But, anyone can clearly see the picture she is reaching for. She is right, but for somewhat the wrong reason. But, our *cognitively dissonant* detractor slams her again. He decided in the beginning, she was *all* wrong, and by golly! *all* wrong she's a-gonna be!

> The intended Hebrew word here is *nedâbâh* (Strong 1890, #5071), which means "free will offering", <u>but it is not a good fit.</u> **And how this relates to a virgin is unknown**...

> [Again, I respectfully decline to name. My emphases, COJ]

Please permit me to answer this way. Imagine, right over there, that we can step through a portal in Time...and we come out in 33 AD, at the foot of Cavalry's awful Cross. Jesus has just yielded up the ghost, and His head bounces dead on His bloody chest, as we step through. That woman, standing next to us, the one who just started howling so piteously, with the tears pouring off her face, is His Mother. Let us step over to her, very gently and respectfully, and whisper in her ear, "Virgin Mother, to obey Moses' commandment, what **willing offering** have *You* made unto the LORD, of all manner of work you have done?" Then, let us slowly walk our eyes down her lifting arm, right out past her pointing finger, to that dead body hanging from those nails. Her Baby Boy—Virgin-born, The Woman's Seed. See NOW how...*PERFECTLY*...it RELATES...to a VIRGIN? What better way to tell such a Story, than to shine it with the Stars, through all the nights of time?

The Band, The Southern Cross, Coma. 3 constellations Rolleston, Seiss, and Bullinger felt *compelled by evidence in those star names*—the oldest names being in Hebrew, and found in one of the *historically* oldest zodiacs—to replace three of Ptolemy's list of 48.

Forgive me, but I am going to repeat something here, something of extreme importance. *The entire presuppositional basis* of The Story in The Stars:

> IF there were a Tower of Babel, and IF there were a Confoundation of Language (with one being multiplied into over 100), and IF there were over 400 following years of scattering confusion, and IF there were a Story in the Stars so confounded, and IF that original language was Hebrew and the confounding left many two and three consonant *word roots* in most of those new languages, and IF faithful adherents of that one language were left linguistically untouched, and IF God inspired men of that original language to write those historical facts in a Book of Scripture, and IF God included plot lines and key points of That Story in the Stars *in that Book of Scripture*...**THEN**...the broken fragments of That Story would lie among the shards of that linguistic confoundation, AND there would be tell-tale clues in the Hebrew two and three consonant *word roots* in those broken fragments of star names, AND That Inspired Book of Scripture (and none other!) would be the greatest clue and the surest glue with which to reassemble those broken fragments of star names back into The Story in the Stars.

Just remember one little nudge, about those star names...you know, the names God *Himself* says He gave them?

> Isa 40:26 Lift up your eyes on high, and behold who hath created these things, that bringeth out **their host** [the heavens v22, hence stars] by number: **he calleth them all** by **names** by the greatness of his might, for that he is strong in power; **NOT ONE FAILETH**.

"Not one faileth". One of the primary arguments of the detractors of The Story in the Stars is to argue that Rolleston was wrong about Hebrew being the Original Language (we've settled that), and therefore she (with Seiss and Bullinger) just scrabbled around and made up some star names from residual evidence that didn't actually *say* it. God said about those stars and the names He gave them, "Not one faileth". Doesn't that *necessarily imply* ("not one faileth"), that in the broken and residual pieces of star names left over from that Babelized Confusion, that one *should* be able to fit *some* of those pieces back together into *those* original star names?

Were Rolleston, Seiss, and Bullinger *perfect* in their restoration of those 3 missing constellations? I seriously doubt it. BUT... were Rolleston, Seiss, and Bullinger *much closer* in their restoration of those 3 missing constellations than was Ptolemy? I believe so.

QUESTIONS ABOUT MEANINGS OF STAR NAMES

First, reread above the argument that Hebrew was the Original Language (from Creation to the Tower of Babel). Second, recall Rolleston's error that the language *but not the vocabulary* was changed at Babel. Gen 11:1 states there was one language and one vocabulary, and vss. 2-9 makes it *implicitly* clear that *both* were confounded at Babel. As we saw, the Jewish linguist Mozeson argues that there are two and three consonant *word roots* of the original Hebrew found in the languages of mankind, and points out over 22,000 such in English alone. These are not *homophones*, as Rolleston's detractors frequently claim.

> **homophone**. Each of two or more words having the same pronunciation but different meanings, origins, or spelling, e.g., *new* and *knew*.   [Oxford American Dictionary]

That would be Rolleston's error of assuming actual words from the original vocabulary had survived. Of course, some did, and were used and translated back and forth in that 400 year Confoundation after Babel. More correctly, Mozeson and others argue for *word roots* survival, and *not* necessarily with unchanged pronunciation. These two and three consonant *word roots* from the original Hebrew would certainly allow at least *partial* verbal reconstruction of at least *cognates* of many original Hebrew names. *That is what I argue in this book*, despite any differing ideas of Rolleston, Seiss, and Bullinger to the contrary. I am *not* defending their many errors, nor necessarily their every correct method. *I am telling The Story in The Stars*...and sometimes, I think some points can be told in a better way.

Did Rolleston et al goober here and there, especially when looking for *fallaciously conceived unchanged Hebrew words*? Yes, indeed. Are the detractors correct on occasion to yell, "Goober!", and to dance and point? Certainly. But, that isn't The Question. Well then, you might ask, "What *is* The Question?"

The Question...to ask the detractors, *especially* when they reject and ridicule possible references to Hebrew names and cognates...

THE QUESTION IS:
> Can you *prove*...in *every* case...when you reject any Hebrew names or cognates of star names, that there is NOT a two or three consonant Hebrew *word root* involved, resulting from the Tower of Babel linguistic Confusion?

They can...*only if*...ONLY IF...if they stick to their *assumption* that Hebrew was *not* the Original Language. But, I have proven from the King James Bible, and its underlying Masoretic Hebrew text, that Hebrew *was* the Original Language. With that in mind, please read one more time (p. 34), *The entire presuppositional basis* of The Story in The Stars. Then, mull it over for a couple of minutes.

When studying the available evidence for The Story in The Stars, I *always* consider that *presuppositional basis* when dealing with star names. Why? Because, as I showed you, I have *proven* the 7 assumptions upon which The Story rests (but which the detractors deny). Whenever I seriously consider possibilities which sometimes involve *mighta-coulda-woulda*, I like to have both feet planted on things proven. It comfortably narrows the choices.

Here is a fascinating place to plant both feet. Richard A. Proctor, in his book *Myths and Marvels of Astronomy* (1877), pointed out that some portions of the 48 constellations of Ptolemy are not visible above the southern horizon. Calculating from the procession of the equinoxes, and when and where those portions *would have* been visible, he concluded *best visibility* would have been between the 30° and 38° N latitude, some time at or before the 22nd century BC. In other words, he estimated the Zodiac as we have it probably originated *at or before the time and place of The Tower of Babel* (the *original* information *could* have come off Noah's Ark, about a century earlier, *in Hebrew*). Now, couple that with a linguistic Confoundation, then toss in over 400 years while folks tried desperately to figure things out...and, Voila!—there is *The entire presuppositional basis* of The Story in The Stars. Both feet, planted solid, on things proven.

Now, I have Another Question. This one for You, Thoughtful Reader.

Is it *possible* that, having tossed The King James Bible *and* the Hebrew Masoretic text *and* the Greek Textus Receptus; then having embraced the corrupted New Revised 'bibles', proffered by The Roman Catholic Jesuits in various forms since 1540 (and especially since mid-20th century, based on the demonstrably corrupt Roman Catholic manuscripts Aleph, B, Alexandrinus, Vaticanus, and Sinaiticus)...IS IT *POSSIBLE*, I ask...that The Story of The Stars is simply no longer IN the New Revised 'bibles' from The Jesuits, nor IN those corrupted Roman Catholic manuscripts used in those new revisions? Is IT POSSIBLE...that is WHY almost all professing Christians who have rejected The King James Bible *also* reject The Story in The Stars?

Hhmmm?

ROLLESTON'S INTERPRETATION OF THE STAR OF BETHLEHEM

The Story in The Stars says nothing about any stars connected with the birth of Christ. It does tell the story of a virgin birth, but it is not connected with stars, per se. However, in the New Testament, the Book of Revelation *does* connect the Birth of Christ with the constellation Virgo, the Sun, and the Moon, to help date that birth.

> Rev 12:1-2 And there appeared a great wonder in heaven; a **woman** <u>clothed with the **sun**</u>, and <u>the **moon** under her feet</u>, and <u>upon her head a crown of twelve **stars**</u>: 2 And <u>she being with child cried, travailing in birth, and pained to be delivered</u>.

Rolleston, for some reason not made clear, even though it had nothing to do with the Zodiac directly, decided to comment upon the Star that appeared at the Birth of Christ. She coupled it with the Coming of the Magi, the Three Wise Men, to Jerusalem. Seiss and Bullinger jumped in. Our favorite detractor could not resist joining them. He said,

> How credible is this explanation of the star of Bethlehem? Unfortunately, it is not credible.

He is exactly correct in his assessment—the Rolleston, Seiss, Bullinger explanation of the Star of Bethlehem is quite mistaken. So, why am I fooling with it, since it isn't a part of The Story in the Stars? Because the Birth *does* involve the constellation Virgo, the Sun, the Moon, and Mazzaroth in his seasons...in a fascinating way. How? So glad you asked, because this is really neat.

Remember when God created the lights in the heavens, that He said, "Let them be for <u>signs</u>, and for <u>seasons</u>, and for <u>days</u>, and <u>years</u>:" (Gen 1:14). Using the constellation Virgo, the Sun, the Moon, and Mazzaroth in his seasons, we are able to calculate the year, the season, the day, and almost the hour that Christ was born!

The following information is adapted, in extremely brief form, from a book I wrote entitled ***The Ever War*** (go internet to "lulu.com", then choose *Shop*, then type *Conrad Jarrell*; also on Amazon), from Chapter 10...where I deal in part with the Birth of Christ and these very astronomical signs we are discussing. There is an even better book on these astronomical signs, which I used to write mine. **The Birth of Christ Recalculated**, by Ernest L. Martin, fbr publishing, 1978. Martin was a meteorologist, and later a minister in Armstrong's Worldwide Church of God. Armstrongism plays little part in this book, but I forbear to recommend most of Martin's other writings. This is the most thorough book I have yet found dealing with the amazing array of astronomical signs that preceded the Birth of Christ. All credit to Martin, for his excellent work in this area.

We begin with the Prophecy of 70 Weeks, that the angel Gabriel gave to Daniel (Dan 9:20-27). We will use a shortened portion here. Please pay *close* attention to my emphases, they will save us a *huge* amount of time.

> Dan 9:25-27 Know therefore and understand, that **from the going forth of the commandment to restore and to build Jerusalem** [cp Neh 2:1-8, 13,17; ie, 455 BC] **unto the Messiah the Prince** [John baptized Jesus spring of 29 AD] shall be seven weeks, and threescore and two weeks: [69 weeks or 483 yrs] the street shall be built again, and the wall, even in troublous times.
>
> 26 And after threescore and two weeks **shall Messiah be cut off** [Christ crucified], but not for himself: and the people of the prince that shall come shall destroy the city and the sanctuary; and the end thereof shall be with a flood, and unto the end of the war desolations are determined. 27 And **he shall confirm the covenant with many for one week: and in the midst of the week** [after 3-1/2 yrs] **he shall cause the sacrifice and the oblation to cease** [by the sacrifice of Himself, spring 33 AD; Heb 9:11-15 & Temple Veil was rent from top to bottom— Heb 9:8 cp with Matt 27:51, Mark 15:38, Lk 23:45], **and for the overspreading of abominations he shall make it desolate, even until the consummation** [the last 3-1/2 yrs, Siege of Jerusalem], **and that determined shall be poured upon the desolate** [Destruction of Jerusalem, 70AD].

Note the active noun "Messiah" in v26, and the relative pronoun "he" repeated 3 times in v27. Hebrew *grammar*, taken *literally*, assures us that the relative pronoun "he" *relates* to the *only acting noun* "Messiah". Jesus did not enter into His Priestly Office of Messiah until He *came out of the water* baptized by John the Baptist. The 483 years foretold by Gabriel ended at that point, 29 AD (add 1, because there is no 0 BC). Then followed 3-1/2 years of ministry, the Crucifixion ("in the midst of the week"), and the 3-1/2 year war ending with the expulsion of Israel from the Land in 70 AD ("the consummation"..."poured upon the desolate"). The extra years between 33 AD and 70 AD are added in by the 40 years of miracles (both to end Israel and begin the Church), which Christ initiated by changing water to wine at the beginning of His first year of ministry (John 2:11, cp. Act 7:36-38).

Notice one important fact: In every language known to man, the 69th week *precedes* the 70th, and the 70th week *follows* the 69th—*such numbering is sequential*. ESPECIALLY when you have an active noun and relative pronouns that *set the bounds*. In order for Satan to use his damnable heresy (2 Pet 2:1) of Dispensationalism, to steal this prophecy from Christ, he first had to *ignore* the active noun "Messiah", then *dream up* the ungrammatical stupidity that the relative pronoun "he" really meant "Antichrist", *although that word appears nowhere in the Old Testament*. Then, he sticks the 70th week *thousands* of years into the future (way, way after week 69), after some imaginary millennium first dreamed up by Emperor Constantine's sycophant Lactantius in the 3rd century—*235 years AFTER the 70th week was FINISHED*. This fecal foolishness first appears in the doctrinal drivel of the Jesuit Lacunza and the heretic Darby (see Dispensationalism, pp. 15-16). Chuck it...then flush it.

The Wise Men (Magi) became involved as the end of the first 69 Weeks (483 years) approached. They knew of the prophecy, because Daniel had been appointed their chief (Dan 2:48), and no doubt explained it to their forbears. The Roman historians Suetonius and Tacitus, living in the 1st century, both recorded that in the East, about that time, it was believed a King would be born to the Jews, and would rule the world. As those first 69 weeks approached an end, some truly surprising things happened in the heavens.

As I wrote in *The Ever War*, on p. 156,

> In Aug 3 BC ending on 25 Dec 2 BC, some fascinating interactions were seen between Jupiter and Venus, and by Jupiter itself. On 12 August 3 BC, a fascinating astral event occurred: About an hour and 20 minutes before sunrise, Jupiter rose in conjunction with Venus as the Morning Star. Biblically, Jesus identifies Himself as the Morning Star (Rev 22:16), likewise Peter (2 Pet 1:19). For the Persians, Jupiter was Father of the gods and Venus was Ishtar, Mother Goddess of Fertility; so the two, in conjunction rising together, as the Morning Star was *extremely* significant. On 17 Jun 2 BC, another more dramatic conjunction of the two occurred, visible westward from Babylon. <u>Venus, now in her alternate role as Evening Star, moved into such a tight conjunction with Jupiter that those two brightest stars appeared as *one* supremely bright star.</u> This conjunction occurred *within the constellation of Leo the Lion, the King, the Lion of the tribe of Judah!* There was nothing like it before or after, not for many generations.

The Magi most likely were guided by Jupiter, as their King star, and followed it westward to Jerusalem. Jupiter appears to move in an ellipsis thru the heavens. As it halts and appears to turn back at the apogee, it seems to hang motionless for a short while. On 25 Dec 2 BC, the King star Jupiter, viewed from Jerusalem, would have appeared to hang motionless in the sky over Bethlehem, *for 6 days.*

> Matt 2:9b-11a ...And, lo, **the star, which they saw in the east, <u>went before them</u>, <u>till it came and stood over where the young child was.</u>** 10 When they saw the star, they rejoiced with exceeding great joy. 11 And when they were come into the house, they saw the young child with Mary his mother, and fell down, and worshipped him...

There is more told in my book, and much more by Martin in his. I encourage you to read them. Bare bones for now—this information, together with John being 30 years old, tells us he started his ministry in 29 BC; which Luke confirms was "the fifteenth year of the reign of Tiberius Caesar" (Luke 3:1-3). These calculations *confirm each other*.

Now, let's skip to that constellation Virgo.

> Rev 12:1-2,5 And there **appeared** a great wonder in heaven; **a woman clothed with the sun, and the moon under her feet**, and upon her head a crown of twelve stars: 2 And she being with child cried, **travailing in birth, and pained to be delivered**. [A constellation of stars, with specified relationship to sun and moon, at the time of Christ's Birth]...5 And **she brought forth a man child,** who was to rule all nations with a rod of iron: [Pregnant Israel gave birth to the Messiah]...

Virgo is the first constellation of the Zodiac, so upon her head (looking backward along the ecliptic) would indeed be 12 stars (or, Constellations). Now, *at what Time* did the setting Sun pass *through* her body ("clothed with") *and* the Moon rise from *directly* "under her feet"? Virgo is the *only* sign of a woman the sun passes through, and for only 20 days; and on 2 BC, it did so between ~27 August and ~15 September; during that time, the Moon rose *directly* between her feet for 14 hours on September 1 (Jerusalem time); The Bible says "appeared"—the time to *see* stars is *after* the sunset (6:30 pm on *that* day), and the 14 hours ended at 8:30 pm *that* day. So, the Time of Christ's Birth, taking everything *grammatically* and *literally*, from a King James Bible and its underlying Textus Receptus Greek, and with some help from Mazzaroth in his seasons, would be

Christ Born ~ 6:30-8:30 pm, 1 September 2 BC

This is better than anything Rolleston, Seiss, or Bullinger imagined, or the detractors ever thought. See how perfectly this *complements* Genesis, and *underlines* The Story in The Stars?

> Gen 1:14 And God said, Let there be **lights in the firmament of the heaven** to divide the day from the night; and **let them be for signs, and for seasons, and for days, and years**:

In Revelation 12, God is pointing the Finger of Inspiration *directly* at the Sign in the stars, that tells us the Year, the Season, the Day, and almost the hour of The Birth of The Seed of The Woman.

CLOSING THOUGHTS

One detractor, whose opinions we have been discussing, said this among his final arguments against The Story in The Stars.

> The gospel in the stars thesis in not biblical on at least two counts. First, nowhere does Scripture clearly teach that such a message is embedded in the arrangement of the stars....Second, the New Testament refers to the gospel as a mystery, something that had not been previously known (Rom 16:25-26; 1 Cor 2:1-8; 1 Pet 1:10-12). Purveyors of the gospel in the stars would have us believe that many people from ancient times knew the entire gospel story long before the New Testament, but this clearly contradicts the New Testament teaching...
> [I respectfully decline to name. My emphases, COJ]

His first point has been refuted (see Assumption 4—God Named the Stars, and Assumptions 6 & 7—Star Names tell a Story, and God told that Story).

His second point illustrates the theological ignorance that overtakes people who toss the King James Version, in favor of New, Revised 'bibles', based on corrupt Roman Catholic manuscripts. First, let's just quote his verses...but, using a King James Bible, of course. Then, I'll show you the passage that he ignored...again using a King James Bible, (maybe it read *differently* in his New Revised 'bible', and he didn't see it). Here we go.

The Detractor's Gospel Mystery Verses

> Rom 16:25-26 Now to him that is of power to stablish you according to **my gospel**, and the preaching of Jesus Christ, **according to the revelation of the mystery, which was kept secret since the world began, 26 But now is made manifest**, and by the scriptures of the prophets, according to the commandment of the everlasting God, made known to all nations for the obedience of faith:

1 Cor 2:1-8 And I, brethren, when I came to you, came not with excellency of speech or of wisdom, declaring unto you the testimony of God. 2 <u>For I determined not to know any thing among you, save Jesus Christ, and him crucified.</u> 3 And I was with you in weakness, and in fear, and in much trembling. 4 And my speech and my preaching was not with enticing words of man's wisdom, but in demonstration of the Spirit and of power: 5 That your faith should not stand in the wisdom of men, but in the power of God.

6 Howbeit we speak wisdom among them that are perfect: yet not the wisdom of this world, nor of the princes of this world, that come to nought: 7 But **we speak the wisdom of God in a mystery, even the hidden wisdom, which God ordained before the world unto our glory**:

1 Pet 1:10-12 Of which salvation the prophets have inquired and searched diligently, who prophesied of the grace that should come unto you: 11 <u>Searching what, or what manner of time the Spirit of Christ which was in them did signify, when it testified beforehand the sufferings of Christ, and the glory that should follow.</u> 12 **Unto whom it was revealed, that not unto themselves, but unto us they did minister the things, which are now reported unto you by them that have preached the gospel unto you with the Holy Ghost sent down from heaven; which things the angels desire to look into.**

This Gospel Mystery Explained in one Passage

Eph 3:3-5 How that by revelation he made known unto me **the mystery**; (as I wrote afore in few words, 4 Whereby, when ye read, ye may **understand my knowledge in <u>the mystery</u> of Christ**) 5 <u>Which in other ages was not made known unto the sons of men, as it is now revealed</u> unto his holy apostles and prophets by the Spirit; 6 **That the Gentiles should be fellowheirs, and of the same body, and partakers of his promise in Christ by the gospel:**

Remember his objection? "Purveyors of the gospel in the stars would have us believe that many people from ancient times *knew the entire gospel story* long before the New Testament, but this clearly contradicts the New Testament teaching." Purveyors of the gospel in the stars do no such thing. The Story in The Stars does indeed *expand* upon The Seed of The Woman, Who will bruise The Serpent's head, Gen 3:15. It does indeed *expand* upon the Enmity between Her Seed and The Serpent's Seed. BUT...*It NEVER pretends to "tell the entire gospel story long before the New Testament."* That is a *blatant* and *inexcusable* misrepresentation.

The Story in The Stars was *always* and *ever* only a high-point summary of The Gospel. As Paul himself succinctly summarizes it: "In other ages was not made known unto the sons of men *as it is now revealed*...That *the Gentiles should be fellowheirs, and of the same body*, and partakers of his promise in Christ *by the gospel*." That blending of Mosaism, with the Gospel of the Crucified Christ, and gathering into *One* Worship Body, The Church, of all the Redeemed of God, *both* Jew *and* Gentile—*This*, and all interrelated details, was *never before* the New Testament, made fully known to men.

The detractor then asks a truly foolish question:

> Why would we want to return to an inferior, superseded, and admittedly garbled message today when we have the superior message so readily and effectively available?

Why, indeed, would *anyone* want something so...*stupid*? Rolleston, Seiss, and Bullinger didn't. No teller of the Story I ever read did. I certainly don't. But the detractors, so *misled* by their giving up of The King James Bible, thus so entrapped in resulting *cognitive dissonance* (as I have repeatedly shown), cannot even see what is before their two looking eyes—*Look*...the detractor could not even see the 'Gospel Mystery' passage Eph 3:3-5, *which <u>fully explained</u> the Mystery, in other ages not made known to the sons of men!*

Finally, remember *three important facts* that...*underline*...The Story in The Stars. In the Star Version, told by the Patriarchs from Adam to Abraham, told in Names that God gave those stars, *not one of those Names failed* (Isa 40:26). In the *Scriptural* prophetic Old Testament version, started by Moses and finished by the Prophets, told in Words God gave the writers, *not one Word fell to the ground* (1 Sam 3:19). In the *Scriptural* fulfillment New Testament, told in Words God gave those writers, *not one Word shall fail* (Mtt 24:35; Luke 21:33).

Just remember that Hebrew was the One Language. Remember that Linguistic Confusion at Babel. Remember those two and three consonant Hebrew *word roots*. Remember, none of those star Names failed; and in the *Scriptural* versions of the Story, OT and NT, not one of those Words fell to the ground. *That* is why it is possible to stick *most* of that Story in The Stars back together...IF you are using THAT Bible.

Now, let's tell that Story in The Stars...

The Story in The Stars

Starlight, starlight, twinkling bright,
   in the death-black Dark of night;

Showing Story told of Yore
   of The Woman's Seed she bore.

How He came for Bride He loved,
   fought the Serpent, died and rose.

Why He left His Bride so long,
   yet promised sure to Come once more.

Stars now reflect Bride's yearning tears,
   as her Bridegroom's Coming nears.

—Conrad Jarrell

Chapter 3
More Complete
Analysis of the Zodiac

As Rolleston, Seiss, and Bullinger show exhaustively, the names of the 12 major constellations are virtually the same, and those of the secondary 36 constellations nearly so, in all ancient near-eastern nations, *with the Hebrew names being the oldest confirmed*—thus showing THE HEBREW ZODIAC IS THE ORIGINAL, *NOT THAT OF THE PAGANS*. As the geographical distance increases from the near-east (to India, China, then Central America), so do the variations in names. This is to be expected...*if* the original Zodiac came off Noah's ark, from the world *before* The Flood, and was scattered after the Tower of Babel. Those similitudes are *virtually impossible* to account for *any other way*. DUH! [Gibbs slaps Tony upside the head]

The oldest records of the heathen generally support the Biblical account. The Egyptians, Greeks, and Romans ascribed a *divine* origin to the Zodiac. The *Bundahis* of the ancient Parsees gives an account of the formation of the Zodiac and names the 12 signs almost as we have them, and claims them to be the work of Ahuramazda, *The Creator*! In the Chaldean tablets, from the ruins of ancient Assyria and Babylon, a poetic legend of one named Izdubar (supposedly Nimrod) is constructed on the 12 signs of the zodiac, proving that the Zodiac existed at the time of its writing, AT LEAST 2,000 YEARS BC. The Chaldean Genesis is an account substantially the same as the Mosaical account of creation. The fifth tablet relates how God created the constellations of the stars, the signs of the Zodiac, both major (for each of 12 months) and minor, the planets and other stars, the moon and the sun. These tablets are dated WELL BEFORE 2,000 BC.

These ancient records, of various ancient peoples (esp. Egyptian Dendera Zodiac, Chaldeans, and Babylonians), take us back to NEAR THE TIME OF NOAH'S FLOOD IN 2348 BC. Noah himself lived during the latter years of his grandfather Methuselah, who had lived during the latter years of Adam, the first man and the first Holy Prophet—thus, Noah heard The Story in The Stars *from his grandfather...who heard Adam tell It!*

Finally—remembering that the Sphinx indicates that the Zodiac BEGINS in Virgo— starting with the *present* position of the sun at the summer solstice (the longest day of the year), then *calculating backward* 'til the solstice is in *the FIRST degree of Virgo* (which has 30°, p.

34 remember?), we arrive at a **DATE FOR THE ORIGIN OF THE ZODIAC OF A LITTLE OVER 4,000 BC**. This accords *excellently* with Bible chronology, which yields a creation date of 4,004 BC. Can you say, "Amen?" *I knew you could!*

I say it again: THE HEBREW ZODIAC IS THE ORIGINAL...*NOT THE ASTROLOGICAL PERVERSION OF THE PAGANS.*

I'm going to just *lay out* what may be *deduced from* the information sources I gave you. Rolleston, Seiss, and Bullinger show, argue, and prove; so I'm going to leave most of that to them (and they do it *excellently*, despite some serious errors). I'm going to follow Einstein's advice to keep it simple, but not any simpler, and just give you my tabulation of their findings, collated and summarized as seems best to me (based upon research for a sermon series I preached 1989-90, *Bible Astronomy* [1]). Any errors are mine, and I don't hesitate to selfishly claim *all* credit due for them ('cause I'm *real good* at that kinda stuff).

In the following Synopsis, the Three Books of the Zodiac are laid out as major sections. Within each section (Book) are given the Houses of the four Major Constellations of that Book, each with their Minor Constellations (Decans) and bright stars, then finally a Summary of the message of each House. Greek and Hebrew word numbers are from Strong's Lexicons.

AS YOU READ, keep an open King James Bible by your side (because the *revised* 'bibles' have *changed* many of the words, and so they often read...*differently*), and compare the names and meanings of the Zodiac symbols with words in Scripture...and remember, those meanings and names were *the ones God Himself first gave* to the stars, on the 4th Creation Day 4004 BC! That, you see, is why the modern 'bible' revisers *changed* so many of them ("*surely* die"..."*lest* ye die"...See?). Moses was not called of God to start writing down Bible Words until after 1491 BC, *over 2500 years later...and over 4000 years later for the New Testament writers!* Keep these dates and facts in mind as you read, and you should find the correspondences between Zodiac and Scripture...*astounding.* If it seems too incredible to be...TRUTH ("An accurate representation of Reality")...then, please, thoughtfully re-read the Proof from Prophecy (Appendix 1). The Story in The Stars, the Zodiac, is a complex system of multiple PROPHECIES. Therefore, it did *not* 'just happen'...it was *Designed* that way.

*****

---

[1] Available on The Detroit Church website: www.detroitchurch.net. Click on Sermons, and type in "Bible Astronomy".

THE STORY IN THE STARS
"Mazzaroth in His Season"

THE FIRST BOOK—
THE REDEEMER, <u>HIS 1ST COMING</u>

1. **VIRGO**—The Promised Seed of The Woman

   Description: A woman bearing a branch in her right hand and an ear of grain in her left.

   Definitions: Heb & Syriac, *Bethulah*; Arab, *Adarah;* Gk, *Parthenos*—all names mean "virgin." *All* the traditions and mythologies affirm the virginity of this woman.

   Important features:

   Ear of Grain—the brightest star therein is Arab. *Al Zimach*, and Heb. *Tsemach*, both meaning "The Branch."

   Biblical Fulfillment:

   Isa 7:14 Therefore the Lord himself shall give you a sign; Behold, **a virgin shall conceive, and bear a son**, and shall call his name Immanuel.

   Isa 9:6-7 For **unto us a child is born, unto us a son is given**: and the government shall be upon his shoulder: and **his name shall be called Wonderful, Counsellor, The mighty God, The everlasting Father, The Prince of Peace.** 7 Of the increase of his government and peace there shall be no end, upon the throne of David, and upon his kingdom, to order it, and to establish it with judgment and with justice from henceforth even for ever. The zeal of the LORD of hosts will perform this.

   Matt 1:20-23 But while he thought on these things, behold, the angel of the Lord appeared unto him in a dream, saying, Joseph, thou son of David, fear not to take unto thee Mary thy wife: for **that which is conceived in her is of the Holy Ghost. 21 And she shall bring forth a son,** and thou shalt call his name JESUS: for he shall save his people from their sins. 22 Now **all this was done, that it might be fulfilled which was spoken of the Lord by the prophet,** saying, 23 **Behold, a virgin shall be with child, and shall bring forth a son,** and they shall call his name Emmanuel, which being interpreted is, God with us.

John 12:23-24 And Jesus answered them, saying, **The hour is come, that the Son of man should be glorified.** 24 Verily, verily, I say unto you, **Except a corn of wheat fall into the ground and die, it abideth alone: but if it die, it bringeth forth much fruit.**

The Branch—there are 20 Heb. words for 'branch', but only one, *Tsemach* H6780 (the word used in the Zodiac), is used exclusively of the Messiah, and appears 4 times:

Jer 23:5-6 Behold, the days come, saith the LORD, that **I will raise unto David a righteous <u>Branch</u>**, and a King shall reign and prosper, and shall execute judgment and justice in the earth. 6 In his days Judah shall be saved, and Israel shall dwell safely: and this is his name whereby he shall be called, THE LORD OUR RIGHTEOUSNESS.

Zec 3:8 Hear now, O Joshua the high priest, thou, and thy fellows that sit before thee: for they are men wondered at: for, behold, **I will bring forth my servant the BRANCH**.

Zec 6:12 And speak unto him, saying, Thus speaketh the LORD of hosts, saying, **Behold the man whose name is The BRANCH**; and he shall grow up out of his place, and he shall build the temple of the LORD:

Isa 4:2 **In that day shall <u>the branch</u> of the LORD be beautiful and glorious**, and the fruit of the earth shall be excellent and comely for them that are escaped of Israel.

Major Stars: *Zavijaveh* (face), "The gloriously beautiful" (cp. Is 4:2); *Al Murreddin* (right arm), "who shall come down" or "who shall have dominion" (cp. Ps 72:8), also in Chal., *Vendimiatrix*, "the Son (or Branch) who Cometh."

COMA—The Desire of all nations.
   Description: A seated woman holding a child. This is the *ancient* picture, as found in the Zodiac of Dendera, Egypt (~2,000 BC), now in Paris; the *more recent* one being Berenice's Hair.
   Definition: Heb, *kamahh* H3642; Strong "to *pine* after", Brown-Driver-Briggs to *long* for; hence, "the desired or longed-for One (Psa 63:1). By some related to Heb *chemdah* H2532; Strong *delight*; Brown-Driver-Briggs *desire*, that which is *desirable* (cp. Hag 2:7). Ancient Egyptian, *Shes-nu*, "the desired son."

CENTAURUS—The Despised Sin-offering.
  Description: A centaur holding a spear and piercing a victim. *Located directly over the Southern Cross.*
  Definition: Arab., Chaldaic, and Heb., *bâzâh*, "the despised" (Is 53:3, same word H959). Another Heb. name, *Asmeath*, "sin-offering" (cp. Is 53:10). Gk., *Cheiron*, "the pierced one" (cp Ps 22:16; Zec 12:10; 13:6).
  Important features:
    1. In both Egyptian and Greek mythology, the centaurs were a race of beings having <u>two natures</u>, half man and half horse (cp Lk 1:30-32; Rom 1:3-4; Phlp 2:5-8). They were despised by men and hunted to extinction (cp Is 53:3). In Greek mythology, *Cheiron* was king of the centaurs, renowned for his skill in hunting, medicine, athletics, music, and prophecy. He was *an immortal child of the gods*, was wounded by a poisoned arrow *from heaven* meant for another, yet *agreed to die so that other might live* (cp. Jn 10:15-18; Is 53:4-6; 2Cr 5:21).
    2. As we shall see in our study of Libra, Christ is also the Victim and dies on the Cross by laying down His own life (i.e., slain by a two-natured being, Himself!). Observe that Christ is the Priest (Heb 4:14), the Sacrifice (1Pt 1:18-20), and His body on the Cross is the Temple (Jn 2:18-21).
  Major Stars: *Toliman* (left forefoot), "the heretofore and hereafter" (Rev 1:8).

BOÖTES—The Coming Judge.
  Description: A man walking rapidly, bearing a spear and a sickle.
  Definition: The Gk. name is from the Heb. root *bô'*, "to come," and means, "the Coming One" (see Ps 96:13, same Heb. word H935). Ancient Egyptian, *Smat*, "the one who subdues and rules;" also *Ban*, an older name meaning "the Coming One."
  Important Features:
    1. Spear, a staff or rod with a metal point (cp. 2Sm 23:6-7)—denotes a Conqueror. Cp. the Rod of Iron rule (cp. Ps 2:9; 110:1-2; Rev 12:5).
    2. Sickle—denotes a Reaper, or one who brings judgement and destruction (cp. Joel 3:13-14; Mk 4:26-29; Rev 14:14-20).
  Major Stars:
    Arcturus (left knee), "He cometh" (referred to in Job 9:9; 38:32).
    Al Katurops (spearhead), "the Branch treading underfoot."
    Mirac (right side, below waist), "Coming forth as an arrow."
    Muphride (left calf), "who separates" (cp Mtt 25:31-33).
    Nekkar (head), "the pierced." Another Heb. name is *Merga*, "who bruises."

SUMMARY OF THE HOUSE OF VIRGO—Virgo, the first sign of Mazzaroth, contains *an outline of the entire Zodiac* concerning The Person of The Coming One. Like Genesis, it is the seed plot of its revelation. The Seed of The Virgin shall come, the Desired of all nations, and shall be born of God and have two natures. But when he appears, he shall be despised and rejected of men. He will agree to be smitten unto death by heaven, that others may live, and will yield up his life on a cross. He will return thereafter, in vengeful wrath to destroy his enemies, and reap an awful harvest of doom.

2. **LIBRA**—THE REDEEMER'S ATONING WORK.

Description: A scales. Found in all eastern and most ancient zodiacs, the down scale toward the Scorpion.

Definition: Latin, *Libra*, "weighing." Heb., *Mozanaim*, from *mô'zên*, "the scales" (Dan 5:25-28, balances). Arab., *Al Zubena*, "purchase or redemption." Coptic, *Lambadia* (from *lam* = graciousness, *badia* = branch), "station or house of redemption."

Important Features: The significance of Libra is that it speaks of the *commercial nature* of Divine adjudication relating to defaults and debts, and involving penalties, prices, and payments. All of this is exactly mirrored in the commercial nature of eternal salvation, as shown below in the verses related to star names. Free-willers, work-salvationists, and humanists hate the idea of *a sin debt that none but Christ can pay*, for that means eternal salvation must be by Divine grace.

Major Stars:

Zuben al Genubi (bottom scale), "the price deficient".

> Psa 49:7-9 **None of them can by any means redeem his brother**, nor give to God a ransom for him: 8 (For the redemption of their soul is precious, and it ceaseth for ever:) 9 That he should still live for ever, and not see corruption.

Zuben al Shemali (upper scale), "the price which covers". Also named *Al Gubi*, "heaped up high," speaking of the great value of the price.

> 1Pet 1:18-20 Forasmuch as ye know that **ye were not redeemed with corruptible things, as silver and gold,** from your vain conversation received by tradition from your fathers; 19 **But with the precious blood of Christ**, as of a lamb without blemish and without spot: 20 Who verily was foreordained before the foundation of the world, but was manifest in these last times for you,

Zuben Akrabi (below the bottom scale, toward Centaurus and the Victim), "the price of the conflict".

Rev 5:9 And they sung a new song, saying, Thou art worthy to take the book, and to open the seals thereof: for thou wast slain, and **hast redeemed us to God by thy blood** out of every kindred, and tongue, and people, and nation;

CRUX—The Southern Cross.

Description: The Southern Cross, located directly beneath Centaurus, the dual-natured One who is slaying the Victim. Due to the procession of the equinoxes, it is no longer visible at northern latitudes. IT WAS LAST SEEN IN THE HORIZON OF JERUSALEM *ABOUT THE TIME CHRIST WAS CRUCIFIED*.

Definition: Latin, *Crux*, "cross." Heb., *Adom*, "cutting off" (cp. Dan 9:26).

Important Features:
1. The Cross figures in the sacred signs of the ancient Egyptians, Aryans, Persians, Assyrians, Hindus, Chinese, Kamchatkans, Mexicans, Incas, Scandinavians, Gauls, Germans, and Celts...in connection with giving up or receiving life.
2. *Tau*, the last letter of the Hebrew alphabet, *was formed by a cross in ancient Hebrew*, and means "a boundary mark, a limit, *a finish*".

Dan 9:24 Seventy weeks are determined upon thy people and upon thy holy city, to finish the transgression, and to make an end of sins, and to make reconciliation for iniquity, and to bring in everlasting righteousness, and to seal up the vision and prophecy, and to anoint the most Holy....26 And after threescore and two weeks **shall Messiah be cut off**, but not for himself

John 4:33-34 Therefore said the disciples one to another, Hath any man brought him ought to eat? 34 Jesus saith unto them, **My meat is to do the will of him that sent me, and to finish his work.**

John 5:36 But I have greater witness than that of John: for the works which the Father hath given me **to finish**, the same works that I do, bear witness of me, that the Father hath sent me.

John 19:28-30 After this, Jesus knowing that all things were now accomplished, that the scripture might be fulfilled, saith, I thirst. 29 Now there was set a vessel full of vinegar: and they filled a sponge with vinegar, and put it upon hyssop, and put it to his mouth. 30 When

Jesus therefore had received the vinegar, **he said, It is finished: and he bowed his head, and gave up the ghost.**

3. In the ancient Zodiac of Dendera, Egypt, this constellation has the figure of a lion, its head turned backward with tongue hanging out, *as if in great thirst.*
   a. Christ is the Lion of the Tribe of Judah (Rev 5:5).
   b. He suffered great thirst on the Cross as He died (see above, John 19:28-30).
   c. The hieroglyphic name attached to the lion meant "pouring water".

   Psa 22:14-22 **I am poured out like water**, and all my bones are out of joint: my heart is like wax; it is melted in the midst of my bowels. 15 My strength is dried up like a potsherd; and my tongue cleaveth to my jaws; and thou hast brought me into the dust of death. 16 For dogs have compassed me: the assembly of the wicked have enclosed me: **they pierced my hands and my feet.** 17 I may tell all my bones: they look and stare upon me. 18 **They part my garments among them, and cast lots upon my vesture.**

   19 But be not thou far from me, O LORD: O my strength, haste thee to help me. 20 Deliver my soul from the sword; my darling from the power of the dog. 21 Save me from the lion's mouth: for thou hast heard me from the horns of the unicorns.

   22 I will declare thy name unto my brethren: in the midst of the congregation will I praise thee.

   Note—*My God*, Folks...you can't make this stuff up! BUT GOD CAN!

4. The Southern Cross is in the lowest part of the heavens opposite North (cp. Ps 75:6-7).
5. ON the Cross of Calvary, just as OVER the Southern Cross, a Person with Two Natures slew a Victim (Himself) by yielding up His own life.

VICTIMA—The Slain Victim.
   Description: An animal being slain by the Centaur, over the Southern Cross.
   Definition: Latin *Victima*, Gk. *Thera* —both meaning "beast."
   Heb. *Asedah*, Arab. *Asedaton*—both meaning "to be slain."
   Important Features:
   1. The Victim is slain by Centaurus, the one having two natures. Jesus Christ submitted to crucifixion, but yielded up his own life (cp. Jn 10:15-18; 19:30, above; Heb 9:14,26).

2. In the ancient Dendera Egypt Zodiac, this constellation is pictured as a little child with a finger on his lips, named *Sura*, "The Lamb"!

Isa 53:7 He was oppressed, and he was afflicted, yet **he opened not his mouth: he is brought as a <u>lamb</u> to the slaughter, and as a <u>sheep</u> before her shearers is dumb, so <u>he openeth not his mouth</u>**.

John 1:29 The next day John seeth Jesus coming unto him, and saith, **Behold the Lamb of God**, which taketh away the sin of the world.

Matt 27:13-14 Then said Pilate unto him, Hearest thou not how many things they witness against thee? 14 **And he answered him to never a word**; <u>insomuch that the governor marvelled greatly.</u>

3. This is the Seed of the Woman, Who will come as a child, and suffer and die, upon a Cross (cp Phlp 2:5-11).

CORONA—The Northern Crown.
Description: The Northern Crown. Nearby constellations: A huge *Serpent* is trying to stick its head into the Northern Crown, but is struggling in the grip of a *Powerful Man* keeping it from doing so, whose *right foot* is upon the *head* of a *giant scorpion*, which is stinging him *in the left heel*.
Definition: Heb. 'ăṭârâh H5850, "royal crown."
Important Features:
1. In the Zodiac, The Cross is followed *immediately* by The Crown (Heb 2:9 + Rev 5:12; Act 2:29-36; Rev 3:21).

Heb 2:9 But we see Jesus, who was made a little lower than the angels for **the suffering of death, crowned with glory and honour**; that he by the grace of God should taste death for every man. (cp. Rev 5:12)

2. The Crown shines *every* night at midnight, *directly* over Jerusalem. As the Believing Jews say about Messiah Coming, "Maybe next year, in Jerusalem."
Major Stars: *Al Phecca*, "the Shining One" (Christ *after* the Cross, resurrected in Glory).

SUMMARY OF THE HOUSE OF LIBRA—The Scales demand a debt payment that no one can make, but that shall be made by the death of a Victim upon a Cross, at the hands of a Person with Two Natures, and the Victim immediately receives a Crown. An incredibly precise summary of the Atoning work of Christ!

3. SCORPIO—The Redeemer's Conflict.

Description: A huge scorpion trying to sting the foot of a man [*Ophiucus*, see next constellation] who has his other foot on its head.

Definition: Arabic and Syriac *Al Akrab,* "scorpion," but also "wounding, war, conflict." Coptic *Isidis*, "attack of the enemy."

Important Features: The correspondence with Gen 3:15 and Rev 12:4-5 is unmistakable:

> Gen 3:15 And I will put **enmity** between thee and the woman, and between thy seed and her seed; **it shall bruise thy head, and thou shalt bruise his heel.**

> Rev 12:4-5 And his tail [a Great Red Dragon, v2] drew the third part of the stars of heaven, and did cast them to the earth: and the dragon stood before the woman which was ready to be delivered, **for to devour her child as soon as it was born. 5 And she brought forth a man child**, who was to rule all nations with a rod of iron: and her child was caught up unto God, and to his throne.

Major Stars:
1. *Antares* (body of the scorpion), "wounding, cutting, tearing." It shines with a deep red light.
2. *Lesath* (in the sting), "the perverse."

OPHIUCUS—A Powerful Man struggling with a Serpent.

Description: A powerful man, holding a huge struggling serpent trying to stick its head into the Northern Crown.

Definition: The Gk name is *derived from the Hebrew*, which means "the serpent held." In the Dendera Zodiac, the man sits upon a throne, and is named *Api-bau,* which means "the chief who cometh." He has a hawk's head (the enemy and killer of serpents). The serpent is named *Khu,* "the ruled, or the enemy."

Important Features:
1. Christ has power to bind the Serpent.

> Heb 2:14-15 Forasmuch then as the children are partakers of flesh and blood, he also himself likewise took part of the same; **that through death he might destroy him that had the power of death, that is, the devil;** 15 And deliver them who through fear of death were all their lifetime subject to bondage.

> Matt 12:28-29 But if **I cast out devils by the Spirit of God**, then the kingdom of God is come unto you. 29 Or else how can one enter into a strong man's house, and spoil his goods, except he first bind the strong man? and then he will spoil his house.

Rev 20:1-3 And **I saw an angel come down from heaven,** having the key of the bottomless pit and a great chain in his hand. 2 **And he laid hold on the dragon, that old serpent, which is the Devil, and Satan, and bound him a thousand years, 3 And cast him into the bottomless pit, and shut him up, and set a seal upon him**, that he should deceive the nations no more, till the thousand years should be fulfilled: and after that he must be loosed a little season.

2. Christ gives us a measure of His power over Satan.

Luk 10:18-19 And he said unto them, **I beheld Satan as lightning fall from heaven. 19 Behold, I give unto you power to tread on serpents and scorpions, and over all the power of the enemy: and nothing shall by any means hurt you**.

Rom 16:20 And **the God of peace shall bruise Satan under your feet shortly.** The grace of our Lord Jesus Christ be with you. Amen.

Major Stars:
Ras al Hagus (man's head), "the head of him who holds."
Saiph (man's right foot), "bruised."
Triophas, "treading under foot."
Carnebus, "the wounding."
Megeros, "contending."

SERPENS—A huge Serpent, struggling with a Powerful Man.
Description: A huge serpent, trying to stick its head into the Northern Crown, struggling in the grip of a powerful man keeping it from doing so.
Important Features: The important point is the struggle for the Crown, *the Contest for Dominion.* The Serpent desires the power of Godhead (Is 14:12-14), and usurped dominion over the earth by Adam's sin (Gen 1:26-28 + Rom 6:16), but was defeated by Christ, Who freed his captives (Heb 2:14-15).
Major Stars:
Unuk (serpent's neck), "encompassing" (cp 1Jn 5:19). Another name is *Alyah*, "the accursed."
Cheleb or *Chelbalrai* (serpent's jaw), "the serpent enfolding" (cp Rev 12:9).

HERCULES— A mighty man, down on one knee, contending with a Monster.
Description: A mighty man, down on one knee, with his right heel uplifted as if wounded, and his left foot firmly set upon the head of the constellation of Draco, the Great Dragon. He has a

great club in one hand, and grips a three-headed monster in the other.

Definition: Arabic *Al Giscale,* "the strong one." The three-headed monster is *Cerebus,* the guardian of the gates of Hell. In the Dendera Zodiac, his name is *Bau,* "he who cometh."

Important Features: The message of this constellation is the Strong One who cometh to tread the Serpent underfoot and bruise its head. Again, the correspondence with Gen 3:15 is striking. See also the promise of God to Christ in Ps 91:11-13.

Gen 3:15 And I will put **enmity** between thee and the woman, and between thy seed and her seed; **it shall bruise thy head, and thou shalt bruise his heel.**

Psa 91:11-13 For **he shall give his angels charge over thee, to keep thee in all thy ways.** 12 They shall bear thee up in their hands, lest thou dash thy foot against a stone. 13 **Thou shalt tread upon the lion and adder: the young lion and the dragon shalt thou trample under feet.**

Major Stars:
Ras al Gethi (man's head), "the head of him who bruises."
Kornephorus (right arm pit), "the Branch kneeling."
Marsic (right elbow), "the wounding."
Ma'asyn (left upper arm), "the sin offering."
Caiam or *Guiam* (right forearm), "punishing." In Arabic, "treading under foot."

SUMMARY OF THE HOUSE OF SCORPIO—The Scorpion is the Great Enemy of the Seed of the Woman, the Serpent, and shall bruise His heel even as the Man bruises his head. The struggle between the two is for dominion, and the Serpent seeks to wear the Crown, but is prevented by the Man, who overcomes him in great struggle. The Man, the Strong One Who Cometh, shall bruise the Serpent's head. A more precise summary of the struggle between Christ and Satan cannot be summed.

4. SAGITTARIUS—THE CENTAUR BATTLING THE SCORPION

Description: A centaur (two natures) armed with a bow and arrow, aiming directly at the heart of The Scorpion.

Definition: Latin "the archer." Heb. and Syriac name is *Kesith,* and the Gk. *Toxotes,* all meaning "the archer." In the Dendera Zodiac, he is named *Pi-maere,* "graciousness or beauty of the appearing"; the characters under his hind foot mean "he conquers."

Important Features:
1. This centaur is identified with *Centaurus*, being named *Cheiron*.

2. A comparison of this sign and its names with the triumph of Christ (Who was both God and Man) described in the Bible is startling.

Rev 6:2 And I saw, and behold **a white horse**: and **he that sat on him had a bow**; and <u>a crown was given unto him</u>: and **he went forth conquering, and to conquer.**

Psa 45:2-5 <u>Thou art fairer than the children of men: grace is poured into thy lips:</u> therefore **God hath blessed thee for ever**. 3 Gird thy sword upon thy thigh, O most mighty, with thy glory and thy majesty. 4 And **in thy majesty ride prosperously** because of truth and meekness and righteousness; and <u>thy right hand shall teach thee terrible things.</u> 5 **Thine arrows are sharp in the heart of the king's enemies; whereby the people fall under thee.**

Psa 64:7-10 But **God shall shoot at them with an arrow; suddenly shall they be wounded.** 8 So they shall make their own tongue to fall upon themselves: all that see them shall flee away. 9 <u>And all men shall fear, and shall declare the work of God; for they shall wisely consider of his doing.</u> 10 The righteous shall be glad in the LORD, and shall trust in him; and all the upright in heart shall glory.

Major Stars:
Naim, "Gracious One."
Nehusta, "the going forth."
Al Shula, "the dart."
Al Warida, "Who comes forth."
Ruchba, "the Riding of the Bowman."

LYRA—The Harp

Description: A stringed harp.

Definition: In the Dendera Zodiac, this constellation is figured as a triumphant hawk or eagle (the Enemy of the Serpent) named *Fent-kar,* "the serpent ruled."

Important Features:
1. The harp is here implies songs of praise for the triumph of The dual-natured Archer over The Enemy, the Great Dragon, and for the work of the Altar (cp Ps 21:1,10-13).
2. The harp was invented during the life of Adam (Gen 4:21) and predated Noah's Flood, so the presence of such a sign presents no problem.
3. The harp is connected directly with praising Christ's work of redemption (see Rev 5:8; 14:1-5; 15:2-4).

Major Stars:
- *Vega*, "He shall be exalted." This star shines with a brilliant white light.
- *Shelyuk*, "an eagle." Arabic *Al Nesr*, also "eagle."
- *Sulaphat*, "springing up, or ascending."

ARA—A Burning Altar

Description: A burning altar, upside down, with its top spilling toward the southern horizon, the area of the heavens the ancients called the outer darkness.

Definition: Gk, "an altar." Arabic *Al Mugamra,* "the completing, the finishing, the making of an end" (see Crux, pp. 41-43—it was *finished* on the Altar/Cross) The emphasis is upon the negative aspect of the sacrifice, the putting away of a curse.
   The Gk word connects directly with the Heb. words *mara* and *aram,* "a curse, an utter destruction." In the Dendera Zodiac, this constellation is pictured as a man enthroned, sitting over a jackal, wielding a flail in his hand. His name is *Bau,* the same as Hercules, and means "He cometh." The symbolism is the same in both figures—the Coming of Judgement.

Important Features: The coming of fiery wrath and judgement, pictured by the flaming altar, has an *exact* counterpart in the Second Coming of Jesus Christ.

Isa 63:1-5 **Who is this that cometh** from Edom, with dyed garments from Bozrah? this that is glorious in his apparel, travelling in the greatness of his strength? I that speak in righteousness, mighty to save. 2 Wherefore art thou red in thine apparel, and thy garments like him that treadeth in the winefat? 3 **I have trodden the winepress alone; and of the people there was none with me: for I will tread them in mine anger, and trample them in my fury; and their blood shall be sprinkled upon my garments, and I will stain all my raiment. 4 For the day of vengeance is in mine heart, and the year of my redeemed is come.** 5 And I looked, and there was none to help; and I wondered that there was none to uphold: therefore mine own arm brought salvation unto me; and **my fury, it upheld me.**

Psa 21:8-9 **Thine hand shall find out all thine enemies**: thy right hand shall find out those that hate thee. 9 **Thou shalt make them as a <u>fiery oven</u> in the time of thine anger:** the LORD shall swallow them up in his wrath, and **the fire shall devour them.**

Matt 25:41 Then shall he say also unto them on the left hand, **Depart from me, <u>ye,cursed</u>, <u>into everlasting fire</u>, prepared for the devil and his angels**:

Rev 19:20 And **the beast** was taken, and with him **the false prophet** that wrought miracles before him, with which he deceived them that had received the mark of the beast, and them that worshipped his image. **These both were cast alive into a <u>lake of fire</u> burning with brimstone**.

Rev 20:10,14-15 And **the devil that deceived them was cast into the <u>lake of fire and brimstone</u>, where the beast and the false prophet are, and shall be tormented day and night for ever and ever**....14 And death and hell were cast into the <u>lake of fire.</u> This is the second death. 15 And **whosoever was not found written in the book of life was cast into the <u>lake of fire</u>**.

2 Pet 3:10-13 But **the day of the Lord will come** as a thief in the night; in the which the heavens shall pass away with a great noise, and **the elements shall melt with fervent heat, the earth also and the works that are therein shall be burned up.**

   11 Seeing then that all these things shall be dissolved, what manner of persons ought ye to be in all holy conversation and godliness, 12 Looking for and hasting unto the coming of the day of God, wherein **the heavens being on fire shall be dissolved, and the elements shall melt with fervent heat?** 13 Nevertheless we, according to his promise, <u>look for new heavens and a new earth, wherein dwelleth righteousness.</u>

DRACO—A Great Coiled Dragon

Description: A great coiled dragon, whose head is being crushed under the foot of Hercules.

Definition: Gk. "trodden on," From the Heb. *dahrach,* "to tread".

Psa 91:13 **Thou shalt tread upon** the lion and adder: the young lion and **the dragon shalt thou trample under feet**.

Psa 74:12-14 For **God is my King of old, working salvation in the midst of the earth.** 13 Thou didst divide the sea by thy strength: **thou brakest the heads of the dragons in the waters. 14 Thou brakest the heads of leviathan in pieces**, and <u>gavest him to be meat to the people inhabiting the wilderness.</u>

Isa 27:1 In that day **the LORD** with his sore and great and strong sword **shall punish leviathan the piercing serpent, even leviathan that crooked serpent; and he shall slay the dragon that is in the sea.**

Important Features:
1. The character of the Great Dragon, as revealed in the meaning of the names in the constellation, *exactly and irrefutably* matches that of Satan, the Great Dragon of Scripture (cp Gen 3:1-7,14-15; Rev 12:3-10).
2. The Dragon is a dominant theme of evil in all ancient European and Near-eastern cultures, almost all Asian cultures, and most African, and North and South American cultures.
3. The last sign in each of the three books of the Zodiac deals with the destruction of Satan: This first book ends with Draco, the Dragon being cast down; the second ends with Cetus, the sea monster, being bound; and the third ends with Hydra, the old serpent, being finally destroyed.

Major Stars:
Thuban (one of the last coils), "the subtle" (cp Gen 3:1).
  About 2,700 B.C. this was the North Star, which is *A SMALL EVIDENCE THE GREEKS DID NOT INVENT THIS CONSTELLATION*.
Rastaban (in the head), Heb. "the head of the subtle." Arabic *Al Waid*, "who is to be destroyed."
Ethanin (in the head), "the long serpent or dragon."
Grumian, "the subtle."
Al Dib, "the reptile."
El Athik, "the fraudulent."
El Asieh, "the bowed down."

SUMMARY OF THE HOUSE OF **SAGITTARIUS**—The two-natured archer, a centaur identical to the one making the sacrifice over the Cross, shall triumph gloriously over his foes, and shall be greatly praised by those that he delivers. He shall finish the judgement against the Great Serpent and his allies, and bring wrath and a great curse upon them to the uttermost.

THE SECOND BOOK—
THE REDEEMED, BLESSINGS PROCURED

5. **CAPRICORNUS**—A HALF-GOAT WITH A FISH'S TAIL.
   Description: In all the ancient zodiacs, the fore-half of a Goat with a Fish's tail. The Goat is bowing its head, as though dying, the right leg folded under the body and the left extended. The tail of the Fish is writhing and vigorous. In the Indian zodiac, it is a goat traversed with a fish.
   Definition: Latin, "goat, and by inference, atonement." Heb. *Gedi*, "the kid, or cut off." In the Egyptian zodiacs at Denderah and Esneh, the name is *Hupenius*, "the place of the sacrifice."

Important Features:
1. Redemption is pictured in the Scripture under the symbol of a slain goat as the sacrifice (cp. Lev 9:3,15; 10:16-17; 16:7-10).
2. God's Redeemed are pictured in the Scripture under the symbol of fishes (cp. Jer 16:15-16; Ezk 47:6-10; Mtt 4:19; 13:47-48; Lk 5:4-10).
3. Christ taught that His death would bring forth life (Jn 12:23-24) and spoke of Himself and His Redeemed as being one (Jn 17:20-23), a theme repeated by Paul (Rom 12:5; Gal 3:28).
4. The Theme of the picture is clear, based upon the ancient names—the Sacrifice would come and be cut off in death, thereby procuring life for those Redeemed.

Major Stars:
Al Gedi (in the horns), "the kid or goat."
Deneb Al Gedi (in the tail), "the sacrifice cometh."
Dabih (Syriac), *Al Dabik* and *Al Dehabeh* (Arabic), all meaning, "the sacrifice slain."
Ma'asad, "the slaying."
Sa'ad al Naschira, "the record of the cutting off."

SAGITTA—An Arrow.

Description: An arrow alone, as if in flight.
Definition: Latin, "arrow." Heb. *Sham,* "destroying or making desolate."
Important Features: The arrow is the instrument with which God pierces His people because of their sin (Ps 38:2, cp Job 6:4; Lam 3:12-13; Zech 9:12-16), thus by implication, He likewise pierced their Great Substitute.

AQUILA—A falling Eagle.

Description: A pierced and wounded Eagle, falling head downward.
Definition: Latin, "eagle."
Important Features:
1. The Eagle in the Bible is a picture of God's care for His Redeemed People (Ex 19:4; Dt 32:11-12). God's Redeemed are pictured as blessed with the attributes of the eagle (Is 40:31; Rev 12:14).
2. The Theme— The Eagle, the natural enemy of the serpent, is pierced and wounded. It is to be identified with The Seed of the Woman, Who is will be wounded in the heel, while doing battle with the serpent.

Major Stars:
Al Tair (in the neck), "the wounding."

Al Shain (in the throat), from a Heb. root meaning "the scarlet covered, hence, covered with blood."
Tarared (in the back), "wounded, or torn."
Alcair (in the lower wing), "the piercing."
Al Okal (in the tail), "wounded in the heel."

DELPHINUS—A leaping Fish.
Description: Most frequently pictured as a leaping fish, head upward. In the Persian zodiac, a fish and a stream of water. In the Egyptian zodiac, a vessel pouring out water.
Definition: Latin, "dolphin." Heb. *Dalaph,* "pouring out of water." Arab. *Scalooin,* "swift (as the flow of water)." Syriac and Chaldee *Rotaneh,* "swiftly running."
Important Features: As the Eagle and the Arrow correspond to the dying Goat, so the Leaping Fish corresponds to the lively Fishtail. Sacrificial death produces the life for the Redeemed (cp the Biblical theme—Lk 24:46-47; 1Cr 15:3-4,19-23; Heb 2:14-15; Rev 1:5-6; 5:9-10).

SUMMARY OF THE HOUSE OF CAPRICORNUS—The dying sacrificial Goat, struck by the arrow of judgement, is the same with the dying Eagle. This sacrificial death is the "wounding in the heel" suffered by the Seed of the Woman in the great struggle with the Serpent. Out of this death will come the resurrection of the Sacrifice and the life of The Rest of Her Seed.

6. AQUARIUS—A MAN POURING WATER FROM AN URN
Description: A man pouring a great stream of water from an urn, which flows downward upon a fish (*Piscis Australis*).
Definition: Latin, "the water bearer." Egyptian *Hupei Tirion,* "the place of him coming down." Heb. *Deli,* "water pot."
Important Features:
1. The correspondence of this picture with certain Old Testament prophecies of Christ and His blessings is striking (Num 24:7; Is 32:1-2; 33:21; 35:1,6; 41:18; 44:3,6 all cp. with Eph 1:3).
2. The Holy Spirit is symbolized in Scripture as water (Ezk 36:25-27; Joel 2:28-29; Jn 4:13-14 + 7:37-39; cp Rev 22:1).
Major Stars:
Sa'ad al Melik (in the right shoulder), "the record of the pouring forth."
Sa'ad al Sund (in the left shoulder), "who goeth and returneth."
Scheat (in the lower right leg), "who goeth and returneth."
Mon (in the urn), "urn."

PISCIS AUSTRALIS—A large Fish.

Description: A large fish, drinking the water poured by Aquarius.

Definition: Latin "The Southern Fish." Arabic *Fom al Haut,* "the mouth of the fish." In the Denderah zodiac *Aar,* "a stream."

Important Features:
1. God's Redeemed are pictured in the Scripture under the symbol of fishes (see Capricornus, Important Feature 2).
2. The man corresponds to the dying Goat Capricornus and the Eagle Aquila, the Fish to the fishtail of Capricornus and to Delphinus, the leaping fish. The Theme—The Blessing obtained by the sacrifice shall *most surely* be poured out upon the Redeemed.

PEGASUS—A winged Horse.

Description: A winged horse traveling with great speed.

Definition: Gk. "horse of the fountain." In the Denderah Zodiac, there are two characters below the horse, *pe* and *ka*. In Hebrew *peka* means "the chief" and *sus* means "horse." *ANOTHER BIT OF EVIDENCE THAT THE GREEKS DID NOT INVENT THE ZODIAC, but rather embellished and distorted what they found already in place.*

Important Features:
1. The names connected with this constellation identify it directly with the Person of Aquarius, the water bearer (which see). Here is emphasized the Certain Return from Afar of the Giver of Blessings. This is a theme concerning Christ in the Scripture (Mk 13:32-37; Mtt 25:14-30; Jn 14:2-3).

   Mk 13:32-37 But of that day and that hour knoweth no man, no, not the angels which are in heaven, neither the Son, but the Father. 33 Take ye heed, watch and pray: for ye know not when the time is. 34 For **the Son of man is as a man taking a far journey**, who left his house, and gave authority to his servants, and to every man his work, and commanded the porter to watch. 35 **Watch ye therefore: for ye know not when the master of the house cometh,** at even, or at midnight, or at the cockcrowing, or in the morning: 36 Lest coming suddenly he find you sleeping. 37 And what I say unto you I say unto all, Watch. (see also Matt 25:14-30)

   John 14:2-3 In my Father's house are many mansions: if it were not so, I would have told you. **I go to prepare a place for you.** 3 And if I go and prepare a place for you, **I will come again,** and receive you unto myself; **that where I am, there ye may be also.**

2. Christ is connected with a horse in some prophecies of His Return.

Rev 6:2 And I saw, and **behold a <u>white horse</u>: and he that sat on him had a bow; and a crown was given unto him: and he went forth conquering, and to conquer.**

Rev 19:11-16 And I saw heaven opened, and **behold a <u>white horse</u>; and he that sat upon him was called Faithful and True, and in righteousness he doth judge and make war.** 12 His eyes were as a flame of fire, and on his head were many crowns; and he had a name written, that no man knew, but he himself. 13 And he was clothed with a vesture dipped in blood: and his name is called The Word of God. 14 And the armies which were in heaven followed him upon <u>white horses</u>, clothed in fine linen, white and clean. 15 <u>And out of his mouth goeth a sharp sword, that with it he should smite the nations: and he shall rule them with a rod of iron: and he treadeth the winepress of the fierceness and wrath of Almighty God.</u> 16 And he hath on his vesture and on his thigh a name written, KING OF KINGS, AND LORD OF LORDS.

Major Stars:
Markab (on the neck), "returning from afar."
Scheat (in the near shoulder), "who goeth and returneth."
Al Genib (tip of the wing), "who carries."
Enif (the nostril), "the water."
Matar (near foreleg), "who causes to overflow."

CYGNUS—A great Swan.

Description: A great Swan flying swiftly.
Definition: Latin, "swan." In the Denderah Zodiac it is named *Tes-ark* meaning "this from afar."
Important Features: This sign emphasizes the swift return of the Redeemer and Judge.

2 Pet 3:8,10 But, beloved, <u>be not ignorant of this one thing, that</u> **one day is with the Lord as a thousand years, and a thousand years as one day....10 But the day of the Lord will come as a thief in the night**; <u>in the which the heavens shall pass away with a great noise, and the elements shall melt with fervent heat, the earth also and the works that are therein shall be burned up.</u>

Rev 22:7,12-13,20 **Behold, I come quickly**: blessed is he that keepeth the sayings of the prophecy of this book....12 And, **behold, I come quickly**; and my reward is with me, to give every man according as his work shall be. 13 **I am Alpha and Omega**, the beginning and the end, the first and the last....20 He which testifieth these things saith, **Surely I come quickly.** Amen. **Even so, come, Lord Jesus.**

Major Stars:
Deneb (body), "the judge." Also *Adige,* "flying swiftly."
Al Bireo (beak), "flying swiftly."
Sadr (body), "who returns as in a circle" (remember Ps 19 —'circuits'!).
Azel (tail), "who goes and returns quickly."
Fafage (tail), "gloriously shining forth."

SUMMARY OF THE HOUSE OF AQUARIUS—The Redeemer shall pour out a river of blessing upon the Redeemed, then He shall go away to a far place; but He shall Return surely and swiftly to Judge His Enemies and Reward His Redeemed.

7. **PISCES**—TWO LARGE FISHES BOUND TOGETHER

Description: Two large fishes bound together by a Band (which is the first decan), the ends of which are fastened to their tails. One fish is pointed toward the North Polar Star, the other along the line of the ecliptic. The Band is fastened to the back of the head of Cetus the sea monster, and the foreleg of Aries the Ram lies across it, between the fishes and the monster.

Definition: Latin "fishes." Egyptian (Denderah Zodiac) *Pi-cot Orion,* "THE FISHES, OR CONGREGATION, OF HIM THAT COMETH." Heb. *Dagim,* "the fishes." Syriac *Nuno,* "THE FISH PROLONGED (BY SUCCESSIVE GENERATIONS)." Arabic and Greek names mean "the fishes."

Important Features:
1. The symbol of the fish *unmistakably* continues the theme of Pisces Australis, Delphinus, and Capricornus (all which see)—this is another picture of the Redeemed, both united with and upheld by the Redeemer.
2. Two fishes emphasize *Duality*, a point clearly stated in the Egyptian and Syriac names. A multitude is indicated (cp Gen 48:16 margin; Ezk 47:9).

Gen 48:16 The Angel which redeemed me from all evil, **bless the lads** [Ephraim and Mannaseh, Joseph's sons, v13]; and let my name be named on them, and the name of my fathers Abraham and Isaac; and **let them grow into** [H1711 *dâgâh*] **a multitude in the midst of the earth.**

H1711 *dâgâh*. A primitive root; to *move rapidly*; used only as a denominative from H1709 ; to *spawn*, that is, *become numerous*. (See next)

H1709 *dâg/dâ'g*. a fish (a*s prolific*).

Eze 47:6,9 And he said unto me, Son of man, hast thou seen this? Then he brought me, and caused me to return to the brink of the river....9 And it shall come to pass, that **every thing that liveth, which moveth, whithersoever the rivers shall come, shall live**: and **there shall be a very great multitude of fish**, because these waters shall come thither: **for they shall be healed**; and **every thing shall live whither the river cometh**.

3. Two fishes also correspond to the fact that GOD HAS TWO CONGREGATIONS—Israel and the Church...*Jew and Gentile* (Is 2:2; Hos 1:10 + Rom 9:24-26; Jn 10:16).

    John 10:14-16 **I am the good shepherd**, and know my sheep, and am known of mine. 15 As the Father knoweth me, even so know I the Father: and **I lay down my life for the sheep**. 16 **And other sheep I have, which are not of this fold: them also I must bring, and they shall hear my voice; and there shall be one fold, and one shepherd.**

    Isa 2:1-3 The word that Isaiah the son of Amoz saw **concerning Judah and Jerusalem**. 2 And **it shall come to pass in the last days**, that the mountain of the LORD'S house shall be established in the top of the mountains, and shall be exalted above the hills; **and all nations shall flow unto it.** 3 And many people shall go and say, Come ye, and let us go up to the mountain of the LORD, to the house of the God of Jacob; and he will teach us of his ways, and we will walk in his paths: **for out of Zion shall go forth the law, and the word of the LORD from Jerusalem**.

    Hos 1:10 Yet the number of the children of Israel shall be as the sand of the sea, which cannot be measured nor numbered; and it shall come to pass, that **in the place where it was said unto them, Ye are not my people, there it shall be said unto them, Ye are the sons of the living God.**

    Rom 9:22-26 What if God, willing to show his wrath, and to make his power known, endured with much longsuffering the vessels of wrath fitted to destruction: 23 And that he might make known the riches of his glory on **the vessels of mercy**, which he had afore pre-

pared unto glory, 24 Even us, whom he hath called, not of the Jews only, but also of the Gentiles?

25 As he saith also in Osee, <u>I will call them my people, which were not my people; and her beloved, which was not beloved. 26 And it shall come to pass, that in the place where it was said unto them, Ye are not my people; there shall they be called the children of the living God.</u>

4. Israel, The Church, & Dispensational Dum-dum Doo-doo [Note: Technical terms *only*; we are discussing Astronomy, Biblical History, and Eschatology]
   a. Dispensationalism argues: Paul (Eph 3:5-9) says the Church was never revealed before his preaching, thus cannot be a subject of OT prophecy.
   b. Dispensationalism refuted: Paul *actually says,* "not made known… <u>as it is now revealed</u>," (Eph 3:5) then states *what was not known*—"that the Gentiles should be **fellowheirs**, and of the **same** body" (Eph 3:6). You see, it was the *unity* of Israel *and* the Church which was hidden, not the existence of the Church.
   c. The *directions the fishes face* are important. One faces North, the heavenly direction (Ps 75:6-7), and answers to the Church, which ever looks heavenward for the *Return* of Him Who Cometh. The other faces along the ecliptic, the path of the sun around the earth, and answers to Israel; which even to this day fastens its attention upon the earth and its promises, and *ignores* that He came the *First Time*...born of a Virgin.
   d. Consider the following names of the Major Stars, "United"and "Upheld", and how they portend Israel and the Gentiles *in the same body* (Eph 3:5-6, see b., above).

Major Stars:

Okada (Heb.), "the United".

> Rom 11:17-18 And if some of the branches be broken off, and **thou, being a wild olive tree, wert grafted in among them**, and with them partakest of the root and fatness of the olive tree; 18 Boast not against the branches. But if thou boast, **thou bearest not the root, but the root thee**. (cp. also Eph 2:13-16)

Al Samaca (Arabic), "the Upheld".

> Isa 41:10-11 **Fear thou not; for I am with thee**: be not dismayed; for I am thy God: <u>I will strengthen thee; yea, I will help thee</u>; yea, **I will uphold thee with the right hand of my righteousness.** 11 Behold, all they that

were incensed against thee shall be ashamed and confounded: they shall be as nothing; and they that strive with thee shall perish.

John 10:27-30 **My sheep** hear my voice, and I know them, and they follow me: 28 And **I give unto them eternal life; and they shall never perish, neither shall any man pluck them out of my hand. 29 My Father, which gave them me, is greater than all; and no man is able to pluck them out of my Father's hand.** 30 I and my Father are one.

THE BAND—Fastening the tails of the Two Fishes.

Description: A long band or bridle, fastening the two tails of Pisces, and fastened to the back of the head of Cetus, the sea monster. The foreleg of Aries the Ram lays across it, between the monster and the fishes.

Definition: Arabic *Al Risha*, "the band or bridle." Egyptian *U-or*, "he cometh."

Important Features:
1. The Band fastens the Fishes to Cetus, but the Ram interdicts the Bondage.
2. The *interrelationship* of the bound Fishes, Andromeda the bound woman, and Cepheus the King (both following) is *inseparable*.

Heb 2:14-16 **Forasmuch then as the children are partakers of <u>flesh and blood, he also himself likewise took part of the same</u>; that through death he might destroy him that had the power of death, that is, the devil**; 15 And deliver them <u>who through fear of death were all their lifetime subject to bondage.</u> 16 For **verily he took not on him the nature of angels; but <u>he took on him the seed of Abraham</u>**.

Hos 11:3-4 I taught Ephraim also to go, taking them by their arms; but <u>they knew not that I healed them</u>. 4 **I drew them with cords of a man, with bands of love**: and I **was to them as they that take off the yoke on their jaws**, and I laid meat unto them.

3. The Band exactly corresponds to the Bible doctrine of Sin, which binds us to Satan until Christ interdicts the bondage with His righteousness, and sets us free.

ANDROMEDA—A helpless Woman, bound by chains.

Description: A helpless woman, bound by chains upon her wrists and ankles.

Definition: Greek, "man-ruler." In the Denderah Zodiac, *Set*, "set up as a queen." Heb., *Sirra*, "the chained," and *Persea*, "the stretched out."

Important Features:
- 1. The chained woman is one with the Fishes, bound to the head of Cetus the sea monster by the Band. She represents the Redeemed, The Bride for whom The Bridegroom is Coming, in His heavenly circuit.

Psa 19:4b-6a ...In them [The Heavens] hath he set a tabernacle for the sun, 5 Which is as a **bridegroom coming out of his chamber**, and **rejoiceth as a strong man to run a race.** 6 His going forth is from the end of the heaven, and his circuit unto the ends of it...

Gen 3:14-16 And **the LORD God said unto the serpent,** Because thou hast done this, thou art cursed above all cattle, and above every beast of the field; upon thy belly shalt thou go, and dust shalt thou eat all the days of thy life: 15 **And I will put enmity between thee and the woman, and between thy seed and her seed; it shall bruise thy head, and thou shalt bruise his heel.**

16 Unto the woman he said, I will greatly multiply thy sorrow and thy conception; in sorrow thou shalt bring forth children; and **thy desire shall be to thy husband, and he shall rule over thee.**

Isa 53:1-3 **Awake, awake;** put on thy strength, O Zion; **put on thy beautiful garments, O Jerusalem, the holy city**: for henceforth there shall no more come into thee the uncircumcised and the unclean. 2 **Shake thyself from the dust; arise, and sit down, O Jerusalem: loose thyself from the bands of thy neck, O captive daughter of Zion.** 3 For thus saith the LORD, Ye have sold yourselves for nought; and **ye shall be redeemed without money.**

Ezek 16:1-9 Again the word of the LORD came unto me, saying, 2 Son of man, cause Jerusalem to know her abominations, 3 And say, **Thus saith the Lord GOD unto Jerusalem**; Thy birth and thy nativity is of the land of Canaan; thy father was an Amorite, and thy mother an Hittite.

4 And as for thy nativity, in the day thou wast born thy navel was not cut, neither wast thou washed in water to supple thee; thou wast not salted at all, nor swaddled at all. 5 None eye pitied thee, to do any of these unto thee, to have compassion upon thee; but thou wast cast out in the open field, to the lothing of thy person, in the day that thou wast born.

6 And when I passed by thee, and saw thee polluted in thine own blood, I said unto thee when thou wast in thy blood, Live; yea, I said unto thee when thou wast in thy blood, Live. 7 I have caused thee to multiply as the bud of the field, and thou hast increased and waxen great, and thou art come to excellent ornaments: thy breasts are fashioned, and thine hair is grown, whereas thou wast naked and bare. 8 **Now when I passed by thee, and looked upon thee, behold, thy time was the time of love**; and I spread my skirt over thee, and covered thy nakedness: **yea, I sware unto thee, and entered into a covenant with thee, saith the Lord GOD, and thou becamest mine.** 9 Then washed I thee with water; yea, I thoroughly washed away thy blood from thee, and I anointed thee with oil.

2. Andromeda means "Man-ruler".

1 Cor 6:2-3 Do ye not know that **the saints shall judge the world**? and if the world shall be judged by you, are ye unworthy to judge the smallest matters? 3 Know ye not that **we shall judge angels**? <u>how much more things that pertain to this life?</u>

Rev 1:5-6 And from **Jesus Christ**, who is the faithful witness, and the first begotten of the dead, and **the prince of the kings of the earth**. Unto him that loved us, and washed us from our sins in his own blood, 6 And **hath made us kings and priests unto God and his Father**; to him be glory and dominion for ever and ever. Amen.

Major Stars:
   Al Phiratz (in the head), "the broken down."
   Mirach (in the body), "the weak."
   Al Maach (left foot), "struck down."
   Adhil, "the afflicted."
   Mizar, "the weak."
   Al Mara, "the afflicted."

CEPHEUS—A King, seated in glory.
   Description: A King seated in glory, crowned and enthroned, with a scepter in his hand, and his foot upon the North Star.
   Definition: Gk, *from the Hebrew,* "the royal Branch;" ANOTHER BIT OF EVIDENCE THAT THE GREEKS DID NOT INVENT THE ZODIAC. In the Denderah Zodiac, *Pe-ku-hor,* "this one cometh to rule." Ethiopian *Hyk,* "king."

Important Features: This King Who Cometh is the Redeemer, and answers to Capricornus. It is He who shall free the Chained Woman from her Bondage.

Major Stars:
Al Deramin (right shoulder), "coming quickly."
Al Phirk (girdle), "the Redeemer."
Al Rai (left knee), "he who bruises or breaks."

> Gen 3:15 And I will put enmity between thee and the woman, and between thy seed and **her seed**; it **shall bruise thy head**, and thou shalt bruise his heel.

SUMMARY OF THE HOUSE OF PISCES—The bound Fishes and the Chained Woman are one and the same, bound to the great monster, but freed by the Redeemer, the Seed of the Woman, Who shall bruise the Serpent's head, then rule as King over all.

8. ARIES—THE RAM, BLESSINGS CONSUMMATED

Description: A powerful Ram, laying in repose, with his foreleg across the Band, between the head of the sea monster and the Fishes.

Definition: "The chief, the head," from *Aryan,* "the lordly." Heb. *Taleh,* "the lamb." Arabic *Al Hamal,* "the sheep, hence gentle or merciful." Akkadian *Baraziggar,* "the sacrifice of righteousness." In the Denderah Zodiac *Tametouris Ammon,* "the reign of Ammon." Syriac *Amroo,* "the lamb."

Important Features:
1. This Book of the Zodiac begins with a dying goat Capricornus and ends with a living ram Aries.
2. Observe how the names of the Major Stars emphasize "the Lamb Who was bruised and slain" (Jn 1:29; Rev 5:6,12).
3. At the time of the <u>Exodus</u> on 14th Nisan, the sun was *newly entered* into the sign of Aries; then, due to the procession of the equinoxes, at the time of the *Crucifixion* on 14th Nisan, was *near leaving* the sign—*just a curious accident?* (cp. carefully Gen 1:14 + Gal 4:4; and Rom 5:6)

Major Stars:
El Nath (forehead), "wounded, slain."
Al Sheratan (left horn), "bruised, wounded."
Mesartim (left horn), "bound."

CASSIOPEIA—A Woman set free, enthroned beside a King.

Description: A Woman freed, delivered, and enthroned, holding a branch aloft in her left hand, sitting exactly beside Cepheus the King.

Definition: "The enthroned, the beautiful." Arabic *Ruchba* and Chaldee *Dat al cursa,* "the enthroned." In the Denderah Zodiac *Set,* "set up as a queen."

Important Features: The correspondence of this picture with the Biblical description of the Redeemed Church as the Lord's Bride is *amazing*!

Isa 54:5-8 For **thy Maker is <u>thine husband</u>; the LORD of hosts is his name; and thy Redeemer the Holy One of Israel;** The God of the whole earth shall he be called.

6 For<u> the LORD hath called thee as a woman forsaken</u> **and grieved in spirit, and a wife of youth, when thou wast refused, saith thy God.** 7 <u>For a small moment have I forsaken thee; but with great mercies will I gather thee.</u> 8 <u>In a little wrath I hid my face from thee for a moment; but with everlasting kindness will I have mercy on thee, saith the LORD thy Redeemer.</u>

Isa 61:10 I will greatly rejoice in the LORD, my soul shall be joyful in **my God**; for he **hath clothed me with the garments of salvation**, he hath covered me with the robe of righteousness, **as a bridegroom decketh himself with ornaments, and as a bride adorneth herself with her jewels.**

Rev 21:9-11a And there came unto me one of the seven angels which had the seven vials full of the seven last plagues, and talked with me, saying, **Come hither, I will show thee <u>the bride, the Lamb's wife</u>.** 10 And he carried me away in the spirit to a great and high mountain, and showed me **that great city, the holy Jerusalem**,<u> descending out of heaven from God. 11 Having the glory of God: and her light was like unto a stone most precious</u>…

Also Isa 62:5; Eph 5:23,25-26 taken with Heb 12:22-24.

Major Stars:
   Schedir (left breast), "the Freed."
   Caph (top of throne), "the Branch."

CETUS—The Sea Monster.

Description: The largest of the constellations, it appears in the drawings as having a great ugly head and a beast's forelegs, but with the body and tail of a whale. The Band (from the House of Pisces) is fastened to the back of its head.

Definition: Latin "the whale," which is a natural enemy of fishes. In the Denderah Zodiac, it is pictured as a great ugly head, trodden underfoot by a swine (a natural enemy of serpents), while overhead circles a hawk (another natural enemy of serpents) crowned with a mortar, the sign of bruising. Its name is *Knem,* "bruising."

Important Features:
1. Based on the meaning of the names of Stars and Constellations in this House, we see a Rebel sea monster, who is an enemy of the Redeemed, overthrown, bruised, and bound in chains.
2. The correspondence of this imagery with the Biblical metaphors of Satan are *extraordinary* (cp. Ezk 28:11-19; Rev 12:1-4,9,17)—see *especially* Perseus, following next!

Rev 20:1-3 And I saw an angel come down from heaven, having the key of the bottomless pit and a great chain in his hand. 2 And he laid hold on the dragon, that old serpent, which is the Devil, and Satan, and bound him a thousand years, 3 And cast him into the bottomless pit, and shut him up, and set a seal upon him, that he should deceive the nations no more, till the thousand years should be fulfilled: and after that he must be loosed a little season.

Major Stars:
Menkar (upper jaw), "the bound or chained enemy."
Diphda or *Deneb Kaitos* (tail), "overthrown or thrust down."
Mira (neck), "The Rebel." A remarkable star, it is quite bright, but periodically disappears seven times every six years, appearing to fade out and in.

PERSEUS—Mighty Man with a sword and a severed head.
Description: A mighty man, with wings on his feet denoting swiftness, holding a great sword overhead in his right hand, and carrying the severed head of an enemy in his left.
Definition: Perseus, Gk. "the breaker;" apparently from the Heb. *pârats. This same word is used of Christ in Mic 2:13*, see below. In the Denderah Zodiac, his name is *Kar Knem,* "he who fights and subdues." The severed head is called *Medusa,* from a Hebrew root meaning "trodden under foot." THESE TWO NAMES OFFER MORE EVIDENCE THE GREEKS DID NOT INVENT THE ZODIAC, BUT ONLY PERVERTED A FAR OLDER TRADITION. In Heb. it is also called *Rosh Satan,* "the head of Satan, or the Adversary." In Arabic, *Al Oneh,* "the subdued," and *Al Ghoul,* "the evil spirit."

Mic 2:12-13 I will surely assemble, O Jacob, all of thee; I will surely gather the remnant of Israel; I will put them together as the sheep of Bozrah, as the flock in the midst of their fold: they shall make great noise by reason of the multitude of men. 13 **The breaker** [H6555 *pârats*] **is come up before them:** they have broken up, and have passed through the gate, and are gone out by it: and **their**

king shall pass before them, and the LORD on the head of them.

Important Features: A Breaker, Who shall destroy the Head of Satan with a mighty sword!

Gen 3:15 And I will put **enmity** between thee and the woman, and between thy seed and her seed; **it shall bruise thy head**, and thou shalt bruise his heel.

Isa 27:1 **In that day the LORD with his sore and great and strong sword shall punish leviathan the piercing serpent, even leviathan that crooked serpent; and he shall slay the dragon that is in the sea**.

Psa 74:12-14 For **God is my King of old, working salvation in the midst of the earth**. 13 Thou didst divide the sea by thy strength: **thou brakest the heads of the dragons in the waters**. 14 **Thou brakest the heads of leviathan in pieces**, and gavest him to be meat to the people inhabiting the wilderness.

Major Stars:
   Mirfak (waist), "who helps."
   Al Genib (right shoulder), "who carries away."
   Athik (left foot), "who breaks."
   Al Gol (severed head), "rolling round." This is also a variable star, fading from bright to dim and back about every 69 hours.

SUMMARY OF THE HOUSE OF ARIES—The Redeemer, though bruised in the effort, shall interdict the Sea Monster's binding power and free the Woman, and then elevate her to a heavenly throne beside the King. In so doing, He shall bruise the Monster's head and bind him with chains.

THE THIRD BOOK—
THE REDEEMER, HIS 2ND COMING

9. TAURUS—THE COMING JUDGE

Description: In all of the zodiacs, the forefront of a huge Bull charging, his horns lowered to gore his enemies. It arises directly out of Aries the Ram. It is also directly across from the Scorpion, so *when it rises the Scorpion disappears.*

Definition: Chaldee, *Tor;* Arabic, *Al Thaur;* Greek, *Tauros;* Latin, *Taurus* —all meaning "bull." Hebrew, *Shur,* from a root meaning both "coming and ruling." In the Denderah Zodiac, there are two names for this constellation: *Isis,* "who saves or delivers," and *Apis,* "the head or chief."

Important Features:
1. Everything here is *centered* on the fact that the Lord is Coming to Judge and to Rule. It is a common Biblical theme that the Lord will come in terrible judgement (cp. Isa 13:9-13; 26:19-27:1; Ps 50:3-6), and the metaphor of goring or pushing with horns is connected with judgement (see Dt 33:16-17; Ps 44:5-8).
2. Note that the Pleiades, the congregation of the judge or ruler, is upon the Bull's shoulder. *Scripture describes Christ, in symbol and clear statement, as bearing His people upon His shoulder.* In the pagan legends, the god Jupiter took the form of a great bull and bore his beloved Europa upon his back across the seas, an obvious distortion of the Biblical theme.

Isa 9:6 For unto us a child is born, **unto us a son is given: and the government shall be upon his shoulder:** and his name shall be called Wonderful, Counsellor, The mighty God, The everlasting Father, The Prince of Peace.

Luke 15:4-7 What man of you, **having an hundred sheep, if he lose one** of them, doth not leave the ninety and nine in the wilderness, and go after that which is lost, until he find it? 5 And when he hath found it, he layeth it on his shoulders, rejoicing. 6 And when he cometh home, he calleth together his friends and neighbours, saying unto them, Rejoice with me; for I have found my sheep which was lost. 7 I say unto you, that likewise joy shall be in heaven over one sinner that repenteth, more than over ninety and nine just persons, which need no repentance.

See also Ex 28:9-12 and Dt 33:12.

Major Stars:
Al Debaran (eye), "the leader or governor."
El Nath (tip of left horn), "wounded or slain."
PLEIADES (star cluster in the shoulder), "the congregation of the judge or ruler;" Heb. *Kiymah,* "the heap or accumulation."
Hyades (face), "the congregated."
Palilicium, "belonging to the judge."
Wasat, "center or foundation."
Al Thuraiya, "the abundance."
Vergiliae, "the center, turned on, rolled around."

ORION—A Mighty Hunter, with a club and severed Lion's head.
Description: A mighty hunter, with a club upraised in his right hand, and a lion's severed head with skin attached upraised in

his left. With his left foot, he is stamping the head of his enemy, Lepus the giant hare. The hilt of his sword is a lamb's head.

Definition: In the Denderah Zodiac, his name is *Ha-ga-t*, "this is he who triumphs;" beneath are characters spelling *Oar*. *The ancient spelling of the name of this constellation was Oarion, which comes from a Hebrew root, 'ôr H216 (see Gen 1:3-5), meaning, "light,"* thus the name Orion *implies* "coming forth as light." ONE MORE EVIDENCE OF THE ANTIQUITY OF THE ZODIAC PREDATING THE GREEKS. The ancient Akkadian name was *Urana*, "the light of heaven." The Hebrew name of this constellation is *kesîyl*, meaning "Fool."

Important Features:

1. Orion *implies* "Light".

    Matt 24:27 For **as the lightning cometh** out of the east, and shineth even unto the west; **so shall also the coming of the Son of man be.**

    See also Lk 17:24; Is 60:1-3; Mtt 17:2; Jn 1:4-9; 8:12; 9:5; 1Jn 1:5; Rev 21:23.

2. The severed Lion's head.

    Gen 3:15 Gen 3:15 And I will put **enmity** between thee and the woman, and between thy seed and her seed; **it shall bruise** [H7779 *shûph*] **thy head, and thou shalt bruise** his heel.

    1 Pet 5:8 Be sober, be vigilant; because **your adversary the devil, as a roaring lion, walketh about, seeking whom he may devour**:

    1 John 3:8 He that committeth sin is of the devil; for **the devil sinneth from the beginning. For this purpose** the Son of God was manifested, **that he might destroy the works of the devil.**

    See also Rev 13:2 + Heb 2:14-15.

3. The root meaning of Orion in Hebrew is *kesîyl*, The Fool. By Substitutionary Atonement, Christ became The Fool.

    Psa 14:1-3 **The FOOL hath said in his heart, There is no God.** They are corrupt, they have done abominable works, there is none that doeth good. 2 **The LORD looked down from heaven upon the children of men, to see if there were any that did understand, and seek God. 3 They are all gone aside, they are all together become filthy: there is none that doeth good, no, not one.**

> Pro 24:7-9 **Wisdom is too high for a fool:** he openeth not his mouth in the gate. 8 He that deviseth to do evil shall be called a mischievous person. 9 **THE THOUGHT OF FOOLISHNESS IS SIN**: and the scorner is an abomination to men.

>4. As the names of the Major Stars tell us, This is the Branch, Who shall come forth as a mighty prince and ruler, to crush the head of His enemy, but shall be bruised in the process—the symbolic correspondence with the Coming of Christ is *unmistakable*.

Major Stars:
>*Betelgeuse* (right shoulder), "the Coming of the Branch." In the movie, Betelgeuse is a devil—*but he gets his head shrunk*—so God has the last laugh! [I just had to say that!]
>*Rigel* (left foot, which is stomping the head of Lepus the Hare), "the foot that crusheth."
>*Bellatrix* (left shoulder), "coming quickly."
>*Al Nitak* (in the belt), "the wounded one."
>*Saiph* (right leg), "bruised;" noun form of the very word used in Gen 3:15 (see above). Like Ophiucus, he has one leg bruised and with the other he is crushing an enemy underfoot.
>*Al Rai,* "who bruises or breaks," as in Cepheus.
>*Thabit,* "treading on."
>*Al Giauza,* "the Branch."
>*Al Gebor,* "the mighty."
>*Al Mirzam,* "the ruler."
>*Al Nagjed,* "the prince."
>*Niphla,* "the mighty."
>*Nux,* "the strong."
>*Heka,* "coming."
>*Meissa,* "coming forth."

ERIDANUS—A great flowing River.
>Description: A great River, flowing from beneath the stamping foot of Orion and the hooves of Taurus, past Cetus the Sea-monster and into the southern sky, the outer darkness.
>Definition: Means "the river of the judge." In the Denderah Zodiac, it is named *Peh-ta-t,* "the mouth of the river."
>Important Features: In some of the ancient legends, the river is connected with fire and destruction. The correspondence with Bible imagery is *striking*.

>>Dan 7:9-11 **I beheld till the thrones were cast down, and the Ancient of days did si**t, whose garment was white as snow, and the hair of his head like the pure wool: <u>his throne was like the fiery flame, and his wheels as burning fire.</u> 10 **A**

fiery stream issued and came forth from before him: thousand thousands ministered unto him, and ten thousand times ten thousand stood before him: the judgment was set, and the books were opened. 11 I beheld then because of the voice of the great words which the horn spake: **I beheld even till the beast was slain, and his body destroyed, and given to the burning flame.**

2 Thss 1:7-10 And to you who are troubled rest with us, when **the Lord Jesus shall be revealed from heaven with his mighty angels,** 8 **In flaming fire taking vengeance on them that know not God, and that obey not the gospel of our Lord Jesus Christ: 9 Who shall be punished with everlasting destruction from the presence of the Lord, and from the glory of his power;** 10 When he shall come to be glorified in his saints, and to be admired in all them that believe (because our testimony among you was believed) in that day.

Rev 20:14-15 And **death and hell were cast into the lake of fire.** This is the second death. 15 And **whosoever was not found written in the book of life was cast into the lake of fire.**

See also Psm 50:3; 97:3; Isa 30:27-28,30,33; 66:15-16; Nah 1:6; Hab 3:3-5; Matt 25:31-46; Rev 21:8.

Major Stars:
    Achernar (river mouth), "the after part of the river."
    Cursa (river source), "bent down."
    Zourac, "flowing."
    Pheat, "mouth(of the river)."
    Ozha, "the going forth."

AURIGA—A seated Shepherd, holding a She-goat and Two Kids.
  Description: A seated Shepherd, holding up on his left shoulder a She-goat which clings to his neck. In his left hand he holds *two* newborn Kids. In his right hand, he grasps a Band or bridle, similar to the one which holds Pisces the Fishes.
  Definition: Latin, "conductor of the reins," hence he is called the Charioteer. *The word is from a Hebrew root meaning "shepherd,"* ANOTHER EVIDENCE THE GREEKS DID NOT INVENT THE ZODIAC.
  Important Features:
    1. The Shepherd.

> Psa 23 **The LORD is my shepherd**; I shall not want. 2 He maketh me to lie down in green pastures: he leadeth me beside the still waters. 3 **He restoreth my soul**: he leadeth me in the paths of righteousness for

his name's sake. 4 Yea, though I walk through the valley of the shadow of death, I will fear no evil: for thou art with me; thy rod and thy staff they comfort me. 5 Thou preparest a table before me in the presence of mine enemies: thou anointest my head with oil; my cup runneth over. 6 Surely goodness and mercy shall follow me all the days of my life: and **I will dwell in the house of the LORD for ever.**

See also Psa 80:1; John 10:11,14; Heb 13:20; 1Pet 2:25; 5:4.

2. The Bands.

Hos 11:3-4 I taught Ephraim also to go, taking them by their arms; but **they knew not that I healed them**. 4 **I drew them with cords of a man, with bands of love**: and I was to them as they that take off the yoke on their jaws, and I laid meat unto them.

3. In his arms—this *identical imagery* is used throughout Scripture (; Jn 10:27-30).

John 10:27-30 **My sheep** hear my voice, and I know them, and they follow me: 28 And **I give unto them eternal life; and they shall never perish, neither shall any man pluck them out of my hand**. 29 My Father, which gave them me, is greater than all; and **no man is able to pluck them out of my Father's hand. 30 I and my Father are one.**

See also Deut 33:27 and Isa 40:10-11.

4. *Two* Newborn Kids, elect Jews and elect Gentiles.

John 10:14-16 **I am the good shepherd, and know my sheep, and am known of mine.** 15 As the Father knoweth me, even so know I the Father: and **I lay down my life for the sheep**. 16 And **other sheep I have, which are not of this fold**: them also I must bring, and they shall hear my voice; and **there shall be one fold**, and one shepherd.

Rom 9:22-26 What if God, willing to show his wrath, and to make his power known, endured with much longsuffering the vessels of wrath fitted to destruction: 23 And that he might make known the riches of his glory on **the vessels of mercy, which he had afore prepared unto glory, 24 Even us, whom he hath called, not of the Jews only, but also of the Gentiles?**

25 As he saith also in Osee, **I will call them my people, which were not my people**; and her beloved,

which was not beloved. 26 And it shall come to pass, that **in the place where it was said unto them, Ye are not my people; there shall they be called the children of the living God.**

Major Stars:
Alioth (goat's body), "she-goat."
Menkilinon (shepherd's right arm), "Band or chain of the goats."
El Nath (right foot), "wounded or slain," as in Aries the Ram and Taurus the bull. See *Aiyuk*, below.
Gedi (marking the kids), "kids."
Maaz, "a flock of goats."
Aiyuk, "wounded in the foot."

Gen 3:15 And **I will put enmity** between thee and the woman, and **between thy seed and her seed**; **it shall bruise thy head, and <u>thou shalt bruise his heel</u>**.

SUMMARY OF THE HOUSE OF TAURUS—The Saviour, who was wounded and slain, shall come as a great Bull, bearing his congregation upon his shoulders, and goring his enemies in judgement. The Branch of the Woman shall triumph over his great Enemy like a mighty hunter, shining with glorious light, and trampling the enemy's Head and destroying it. He shall send forth a River of terrible judgement. Like a tender Shepherd, he will gather his Flock in his arms and protect them.

10. **GEMINI**—TWO-FOLD NATURE OF THE JUDGE
    Description: Two male figures in repose, the one bearing a bow and arrows, the other a club.
    Definition: Latin, "the twins." In the Denderah Zodiac, the name is *Claustrum Hor,* "the place of him who cometh." Coptic *Pi-Mahi,* Hebrew *Thaumim,* and Arabic *Al Tauman* all mean "united."
    Important Features:
    1. In the Denderah Zodiac, the two figures are a man and a woman. Seiss (Gospel in the Stars) thinks that this is Christ and the Church. But the club and the bow are both weapons of Hercules, who is one with Sagittarius, the Centaur archer armed with a bow. *The symbolism is a repetition of the dual-nature theme*, recurring so often in the Zodiac, and the weaponry supports this.
    2. The dual-natured Person—<u>the one on the right is a judge</u> who is set and treading under feet; <u>the one on the left comes to suffer</u> and be wounded (see Apollo and Hercules, Major Stars). These are one and the same with the person who is The Branch and The Seed of The Woman (cp. the

Two Comings of Christ: 1st to suffer as Man, 2d to rule as God).

Phlp 2:5-11 Let this mind be in you, which was also in **Christ Jesus**: 6 Who, **being in <u>the form of God</u>, thought it not robbery to be equal with God**: 7 But **made himself of no reputation, and took upon him <u>the form of a servant</u>, and was made in the likeness of men:** 8 And <u>being found in fashion as a man, he humbled himself, and became obedient unto death, even the death of the cross.</u> 9 **Wherefore God also hath highly exalted him, and given him a name which is above every name: 10 That at the name of Jesus every knee should bow,** of things in heaven, and things in earth, and things under the earth; 11 And that **every tongue should confess that Jesus Christ is Lord, to the glory of God the Father.**

Cp. also Heb 9:28; 12:2.

   3. The Branch (see Virgo, Important features 2).
Major Stars:
   APOLLO (head of <u>figure on right</u>), "ruler or judge."
   Waset (right arm of figure on right), "set."
   Mebsuta (in knee of figure on right), "treading under feet."
   HERCULES (head of <u>figure on left</u>), "who cometh (to labor or suffer)."
   Al Henah (left foot of figure on left), "hurt, wounded, or afflicted.
   Propus, "the Branch."
   Al Giauza, "the palm branch."
   Al Dira, "the seed or branch."

LEPUS—A large Hare.
   Description: A large Hare, *whose head is being stomped* by Orion.
   Definition: Latin, "the hare." In the Persian Zodiac, it appears as a serpent. In the Denderah Zodiac as a bird standing on a serpent. Its name is *Bashti-beki,* "confounded+failing."
   Important Features: *There is no mistaking the Identity of this Enemy*, whose head is bruised in Gen 3:15 (cp. also Ps 60:12; Is 63:3-4).
   Major Stars:
   Arnebo (body), "the enemy of him that cometh."
   Nibal, "the mad".

      Ezk 28:17-18 [To The Anointed Cherub that Covereth, v14] Thine heart was lifted up because of thy beauty, thou hast corrupted thy wisdom by reason of thy brightness: I will cast thee to the ground, I will lay thee before kings, that they may behold thee. 18 Thou hast defiled thy sanctuaries by the multitude of thine iniquities, by the iniquity of thy traffic; **therefore will I bring forth a fire from the <u>midst</u> of thee**, it shall devour thee, and I will bring thee to ashes upon the earth in the sight of all them that behold thee.

midst. H8432 *tavek* = From an unused root meaning to *sever*; a *bisection*, that is, (by implication) the *centre*. [the center of a rational being is the mind, hence a split mind, COJ]

Schizophrenia (lit., "split-mind"). **A long-term mental disorder** of a type involving a **breakdown in the relation between thought, emotion, and behavior,** leading to **faulty perception,** inappropriate actions and feelings, **withdrawal from reality** and personal relationships **into fantasy and delusion**, and a sense of mental fragmentation. [Oxford American, my emphasis COJ]

Rakis, "bound" (cp).

Rev 20:1-3 And **I saw an angel come down from heaven,** having the key of the bottomless pit and a great chain in his hand. 2 **And he laid hold on the dragon, that old serpent, which is the Devil, and Satan, and bound him a thousand years,** 3 And cast him into the bottomless pit, and shut him up, and set a seal upon him, that he should deceive the nations no more, till the thousand years should be fulfilled: and <u>after that he must be loosed a little season.</u>

Sugia, "the deceiver" (cp).

Rev 12:7-9 And **there was war in heaven**: <u>Michael and his angels fought against the dragon; and the dragon fought and his angels, 8 And prevailed not; neither was their place found any more in heaven.</u> 9 And **the great dragon was cast out, that old serpent, called the Devil, and Satan, <u>which deceiveth the whole world:</u> <u>he was cast out into the earth, and his angels were cast out with him.</u>**

CANIS MAJOR—A large Dog.

Description: A large dog, poised as if to leap upon Lepus the Hare.

Definition: In the Denderah Zodiac, it is pictured as a hawk (the natural enemy of the serpent) and is named *Apes,* "the head." In the Persian Zodiac, it is pictured as a wolf, and is named *Zeeb,* which is also its Hebrew name, both meaning "wolf."

Important Features:
- 1. The Ancients associated the star Sirius (see Sirius, below) with great heat. This recalls Eridanus, the river of judgement originating under the feet of Orion, and further serves to associate the symbols as pointing to the same person.
- 2. Remember that the title "leader or chief" (see Muliphen, below) is also characteristic of Ophiucus, Aries the Ram, and Taurus the Bull. There is no mistaking the Identity of this Personage, it is as obvious as was Lepus—He is Christ. This sign emphasizes Christ as The Prince who is Victorious.

Major Stars:
SIRIUS (head), "The Prince." Called the dog-star. In ancient Akkadian *Kasista,* "leader or prince."
Mirzam (left forefoot), "prince."
Wesen (body), "the bright or shining."
Adhara (right hind leg), "the glorious."
Aschere, "who shall come."
Seir, "prince."
Abur, "the mighty."
Al Habor, "the mighty."
MULIPHEN, "the leader or chief."
Al Shira Al Femeniya, "the Prince or Chief *of the Right Hand*" (cp).

Psa 110:1,5 **The LORD said unto my Lord, Sit thou at my right hand, until I make thine enemies thy footstool.**...5 The Lord **at thy right hand** shall strike through kings in the day of his wrath.

Heb 12:2 Looking unto **Jesus the author and finisher of our faith**; who for the joy that was set before him endured the cross, despising the shame, and **is set down at the right hand of the throne of God.**

See also Rom 8:34; Eph 1:20-23; Col 3:1; Heb 1:3; 8:1; 10:12; 1Pt 3:22.

CANIS MINOR—A smaller Dog.
Description: A smaller dog, facing toward Lepus the Hare.
Definition: The Egyptian name in the Denderah Zodiac is *Sebak,* "conquering or victorious." It is shown there as a man with a hawk's head.
Important Features:
- 1. This sign emphasizes Christ as The Redeemer who suffered.

2. Note that as Gemini began with two *persons* in one sign—one victorious, the other wounded—so it ends with two *princes*, one triumphant, the other a suffering redeemer.
3. Above all, the House of Gemini the Twins emphasizes *The Two Comings of Christ*—First, as suffering Redeemer; Second, as triumphant Judge and Ruler.

Major Stars:
Procyon (body), "the Redeemer."
Al Gomeisa, "load-bearing for others."
Al Shira Al Shemeliya, "the prince or chief of the *left* hand." This is the counterpart of Sirius in Canis Major, and relates both to the two male figures of Gemini.
Al Mirzam, "the prince or ruler," as in Orion, thus relating the two as the same person.
Al Gomeyra, "who completes or perfects."

SUMMARY OF THE HOUSE OF GEMINI—The Branch, The Seed of The Woman, He Who has two natures, shall come as both a suffering Redeemer and a triumphant Judge, and he shall bruise the head of the enemy.

11. CANCER—THE REDEEMED POSSESSIONS

Description: A large crab, its feet directly over the head of Hydra, the great serpent. It is the same in the Parsi, Hindu, and Chinese Zodiacs, and in an Egyptian Zodiac found in Rome. In the Denderah and Esneh Zodiacs, and in a Hindu Zodiac dating from 400 BC, it is pictured as a scarab beetle.

Definition: ThisLatin name, the Gk. name *Karkinos,* and the Syriac name *Sartano* all mean "holding or encircling." The Arabic name is *Al Surtan,* which means "who holds or binds;" possibly from the Hebrew root *açar,* meaning "to yoke or hitch." In the Denderah Zodiac, the name is *Klaria,* "the cattle-folds."

Important Features:
1. The names of the constellation and major stars emphasize Someone Who 'holds or encircles' a Multitude of assembled thousands of Lambs. It is not difficult to connect the symbolism with that of Auriga the Shepherd, who holds the she-goat and her kids in his arms (cp Gen 22:17-18 + Gal 3:16,29 + Rev 7:9-10).
2. The Sheltering or Hiding Place, see Acubene, below.

Isa 43:13 Yea, before the day was I am he; and **there is none that can deliver out of my hand: I will work, and who shall let it?**

John 10:27-30 **My sheep** hear my voice, and I know them, and they follow me: 28 And **I give unto them eternal life; and they shall never perish, neither** shall any man pluck them out of my hand. 29 My Father, which gave them me, is greater than all; and no man is able to pluck them out of my Father's hand. 30 I and my Father are one.

3. The Two Asses (see Asellus Boreas and Asellus Australis, below).

Zec 9:9 Rejoice greatly, O daughter of Zion; shout, O daughter of Jerusalem: behold, **thy King cometh unto thee:** he is just, and having salvation; lowly, and **riding upon <u>an ass</u>, and upon a colt <u>the foal of an ass</u>**. (Fulfilled in Matt 21:2-9)

4. Feet of the Crab over the head of Hydra—The One Who holds the multitude shall tread upon the Serpent's head, but also cp. Luke 10:19; Rom 16:20.
5. The constellation emphasizes the successful Gathering of All, for whom the Shepherd has come.

John 6:39 And **this is the Father's will** which hath sent me, **that of <u>all which he hath given me</u> I should lose <u>nothing</u>, but should raise <u>it</u> up again at the last day**. (cp. also Is 53:10-11; Heb 2:10-13)

Major Stars:
Praesepe (a bright cluster of stars in the exact center of the body), "a multitude, offspring."
Tegmine (tail), "holding."
ACUBENE (lower large claw), "the sheltering or hiding place."
ASELLUS BOREAS and ASELLUS AUSTRALIS (two stars north and south of Praesepe), "the northern and southern Ass."
Ma'alaph, "assembled thousands."
Al Himarein, "the kids or lambs."

URSA MINOR—A small Bear.

Description: A small bear with a long, uplifted tail.
Definition: Latin, "the little bear." *It is certain that the picture we have is a later corruption of the original*, since no bears ever had tails such as these. Most likely, it resulted from a confusion of the Heb. *dob* (bear) for *dober* (pasture, hence flock). This is reasonably inferred from the meaning of the Major Star names in *both* bear constellations.
Important Features:
1. The original meaning of the two bear constellations was most likely two flocks or sheepfolds (for reasons explained above).
2. The picture is an assembly of young kids, waiting for their Coming Shepherd.

Tit 2:11-14 For **the grace of God that bringeth salvation** hath appeared to all men, 12 **Teaching us** <u>that, denying ungodliness and worldly lusts, we should live soberly, righteously, and godly, in this present world;</u> 13 <u>**Looking for**</u> that blessed hope, and <u>**the glorious appearing of the great God and our Saviour Jesus Christ;**</u> 14 **Who gave himself for us, that he might redeem us from all iniquity, and purify unto himself a peculiar people, zealous of good works.**

Cp. also John 10:16; Rom 9:23b-24; Eph 3:3-6; Heb 9:28; Phlp 3:20; 1Thss 1:9-10.

3. The Pole Star—When the Zodiac began, the star Alpha Draconis, in the constellation of Draco, was the pole star. Due to the procession of the equinoxes, *Al Ruccaba* is now the pole star. A long, long time...an old, old story.

Major Stars:
Al Ruccaba (the brightest star in the constellation, in the tip of the tail), "the turned upon, or ridden upon." Today, it is the Pole Star.
Kochab (shoulder), "waiting him who cometh."
Al Pherkadain, "the calves or the young."
Al Gedi, "the kid."
Al Kaid, "the assembled."
Arctos, derived from *arx,* "the stronghold of the saved."

URSA MAJOR—A large Bear.
Description: A large bear with a long, uplifted tail. We know it as The Big Dipper.
Definition: Latin, "the large bear." [See comments on Little Bear] In Job 9:9 and 38:32, it's called Arcturus, which translates the Heb. *Ayish,* which comes from a root meaning "to hasten." Arabic *Al Naish,* "the assembled together."
Important Features:
1. There is little doubt the picture here is of a flock of sheep—the meaning of the Major Star names is inescapable.
2. The Little Bear and the Great Bear are a picture of two flocks, and the Great Bear is called *Dubeh Lachar,* "the latter herd or flock.". God has a Jewish flock and a Gentile flock; and the Gentiles, who compose the latter flock, are by far the larger flock (Ezk 34:12-16; Rom 9:24). Repeats the dual theme of the constellation of Pisces.

Major Stars:
Dubhe (in the back), "a herd of animals, or a flock."
Merach (body), "the flock."
Phaeda or *Phacda* (hip), "visited, guarded, or numbered."
Alioth (base of tail), "a she-goat," as in Auriga the Shepherd.

Mizar (middle of the tail), "separate or small."
Al Cor (middle of the tail), "the lamb."
Benet Naish (tip of tail), "daughters of the assembly." Also called *Al Kaid,* "the assembled," as in the Little Bear.
El Alcola, "the sheepfold."
Cab'd al Asad, "multitude, many assembled."
Annaish, "the assembled."
Megrez, "separated (as the flock in the fold)."
El Kaphrah, "protected, covered, redeemed, ransomed."
Dubeh Lachar, "the latter herd or flock."
Helike, "company of travelers."
Amaza, "coming and going."
Calisto, "the sheepfold."

ARGO—A Ship.

Description: A sea-going ship, with a lion's-head facing backward for a prow.
Definition: Means "the company of travelers."
Important Features:
1. The Ship represents the multitude of Travelers, who are the possession of the Branch, the Desired One Who Cometh. This links us back to the Seed of the Woman.
2. God's Redeemed are pictured in Scripture as travelers in a ship.

Psa 107:23-32 **They that go down to the sea in ships, that do business in great waters; 24 These see the works of the LORD, and his wonders in the deep.** 25 For he commandeth, and raiseth the stormy wind, which lifteth up the waves thereof. 26 They mount up to the heaven, they go down again to the depths: their soul is melted because of trouble. 27 They reel to and fro, and stagger like a drunken man, and are at their wit's end.

28 **Then they cry unto the LORD in their trouble, and he bringeth them out of their distresses.** 29 He maketh the storm a calm, so that the waves thereof are still. 30 Then are they glad because they be quiet; so he bringeth them unto their desired haven.

31 **Oh that men would praise the LORD** for his goodness, and for his wonderful works to the children of men! 32 **Let them exalt him also in the congregation of the people**, and praise him in the assembly of the elders.

See also Pro 30:18-19; Isa 60:9.

Major Stars:
- *Canopus* (near the keel), "the possession of him who cometh."
- *Sephina*, "the multitude or abundance."
- *Tureis*, "the possession."
- *Asmidiska*, "the released who travel."
- *Soheil*, "the desired."
- *Subilon*, "the Branch."

SUMMARY OF THE HOUSE OF CANCER—The meaning of Cancer and its decans is that there is One Who treads upon the Serpent's Head and holds a great multitude of Redeemed Ones in safety in His hands. This multitude is composed of Two Flocks, one latter in time and much greater in size than the earlier. They will ultimately travel together in great safety, as in a ship upon the sea.

12. **LEO**—THE REDEEMER'S TRIUMPH

Description: A great Lion, pouncing with its forepaws upon the head of Hydra the serpent. There is no confusion about this sign, IT IS A LION THROUGHOUT—in the Denderah and Esneh Zodiacs of Egypt, in the Indian Zodiacs, in the ancient Persian and Hindu, and the oriental Zodiacs.

Definition: Means "lion." The Egyptian name is *Pi Mentekeon*, "the pouring out." The Heb. name is *Arieh*, signifying a lion hunting down its prey. Syriac *Aryo*, "the rending lion." Arabic *Al Asad*, "a lion leaping forth."

Important Features:

1. In the last book of the Zodiac, the Seed of the Woman appears as a Lion; likewise so, in the last book of the Bible!

   Rev 5:1-5 And I saw in the right hand of him that sat on the throne a book written within and on the backside, sealed with seven seals. 2 And I saw a strong angel proclaiming with a loud voice, Who is worthy to open the book, and to loose the seals thereof? 3 **And no man in heaven, nor in earth, neither under the earth, was able to open the book, neither to look thereon.** 4 And I wept much, because no man was found worthy to open and to read the book, neither to look thereon. 5 And one of the elders saith unto me, **Weep not: behold, THE LION OF THE TRIBE OF JUDA, THE ROOT OF DAVID, hath prevailed to open the book, and to loose the seven seals thereof.**

2. The Denderah Zodiac shows a *composite* of all four constellations of Leo: A lion treading upon a serpent, a bird of prey also perched upon it, while below a female figure holds two cups (see decans following). Underneath are the

hieroglyphics pronouncing *Knem,* meaning "who conquers." By the woman is *Her-ua,* meaning "great enemy."

3. In The Bible, the Seed of the Woman, Jesus Christ, is called a Lion (Gen 49:8-10 + Rev 5:5-7).

Gen 49:8-10 **Judah**, thou art he whom thy brethren shall praise: thy hand shall be in the neck of thine enemies; thy father's children shall bow down before thee. 9 **Judah is a lion's whelp**: from the prey, my son, thou art gone up: he stooped down, **he couched as a lion, and as an old lion**; who shall rouse him up? 10 <u>The sceptre shall not depart from Judah, nor a lawgiver from between his feet, **until Shiloh come**; **and unto him shall the gathering of the people be**</u>.

—taken together with—

Rev 5:5a And one of the elders saith unto me, **Weep not: behold, THE LION OF THE TRIBE OF JUDA, THE ROOT OF DAVID**...

4. In The Bible, the Lord in Judgement is described under the metaphor of a lion or a lion's actions (cp. Hos 13:7-8; Zep 3:8; Isa 42:13-14; Amos 1:2; 3:4,8; Psm 50:22).
5. CONCLUSION: *It cannot be reasonably denied* that there is an *exact* correspondence between the symbolism of Leo and that of the Lord Jesus Christ at His second coming.

Major Stars:

Regulus (the heart of the lion), "treading under foot."
Denebola (tip of tail), "the judge or lord who cometh."
Al Giebha (the mane), "the exaltation."
Zosma (hinder part of back), "shining forth."
Sarcam, "the Joining," subtly indicating here is where the two ends of the Zodiac join.
Minchir al Asad, "the punishing or tearing of the lion."
Deneb Aleced, "the judge cometh who seizes."
Al Defera, "the enemy put down."

HYDRA—A huge Serpent.

Description: A huge Serpent, lying outside the ecliptic, whose head is being trod upon by the feet of both Leo the Lion and Cancer the Crab.
Definition: "The Abhorred."
Important Features:

1. IN THE ZODIAC, the Seed of the Woman repeatedly crushes the head of the Serpent, who wounds His heel. IN THE BIBLE, the Seed of the Woman was prophesied to bruise the serpent's head, and the serpent His heel (Gen 3:15).

2. Further: IN THE ZODIAC, the Serpent is called rebel, deceiver, enemy. IN THE BIBLE, Satan is pictured as a Serpent, that rebels against God and deceives the whole world (Rev 12:3-4,9).
3. Finally: IN THE ZODIAC, the serpent is first bound then destroyed by the Seed of the Woman. IN THE BIBLE, Satan is first bound then destroyed by Jesus Christ, Who is the Seed of the Woman (Gen 3:15; Rev 20:1-3,7-10).
4. CONCLUSION: *It cannot be reasonably denied* that there is an *exact* correspondence between the symbolism of Hydra in the Zodiac and that of Satan in The Bible.

Major Stars:

Al Phard (the heart of the serpent), "the separated or put away."

Al Drian, "the abhorred."

Minchar al Sugia, "the piercing of the deceiver."

CRATER—A Large Cup.

Description: A great cup, fixed firmly to the back of Hydra the Serpent.

Definition: "The cup."

Important Features:
1. Crater is formed from thirteen stars, the number associated with apostasy (Gen 14.4, first mention; 1Kg 6:38-7:1 + 3:3 + 11:1-11).
2. The Cup, in The Bible, is a symbol of God's Wrath in Judgement (; 16:19)

> Rev 16:19b ...**great Babylon** came in remembrance before God, **to give unto her the cup of the wine of the fierceness of his wrath**. (cp. also Psa 75:8; 11:6; Rev 14:10)

Major Stars: *Al Ches,* "the cup."

CORVUS—A Bird of Prey.

Description: A bird of prey, perched upon Hydra's back, and attacking it with its beak.

Definition: "The Raven." In the Denderah Zodiac, *Her-na,* from *her* (the enemy) + *na* (breaking up or failing), hence "the breaking up of the enemy."

Important Features: In the Scripture, the fowls of the air are frequently pictured as *judgement inflicted* (Pro 30:17; vs Goliath, 1Sm 17:46; on Judgement Day, Rev 19:17-18). The fowls of the air picked the flesh from the bones of the slain enemy; therefore, the symbol is one of the *utter destruction* of the great Enemy of the Seed of the Woman.

Major Stars:
- *Al Chibar* (eye), "joining together;" from Heb. H6895 *qâbab* "accursed," as in Num 23:8—hence, "the curse inflicted."
- *Al Goreb* (right wing), "the raven."
- *Minchar al Goreb,* "the raven tearing in pieces."

SUMMARY OF THE HOUSE OF LEO—The Great Lion, Who is the Seed of the Woman, Coming in Judgement, shall crush the head of His old Enemy the Serpent, and utterly destroy him, pouring upon him wrath and fury to the uttermost, and the Raven shall eat the flesh from his dead bones. **And so ends** The Story in The Stars, told by Mazzaroth in His Season.

It will be helpful, at this point, to summarize what we have learned about the Zodiac. After all, we have the benefit of The Bible, Old and New Testaments, and historical hindsight—The Bridegroom has Come, the First Time. But for 2513 years (til Moses began to write), all the Patriarchs had were 12 Major and 36 Minor Signs, and the Names of the Stars. They could not *see* the amazing *correspondences*, as we *now* can. They had only the *Signs* in the stars (Gen 1:14, see p. 6), which told a Story. When we read the Summaries of the Mazzaroth below, *then* we can also see that Story, as they saw it... so far long gone ago, shining there...in the stars. Thus, we have the Best of 2 Worlds—the Story in the Stars *and* the Scriptures of God.

THE ZODIAC SUMMARIZED
"Mazzaroth in His Season"

THE FIRST BOOK—
THE REDEEMER, HIS 1ST COMING

1. **Summary of the House of VIRGO**—Virgo, the first sign of Mazzaroth, contains *an outline of the entire Zodiac* concerning The Person of The Coming One. Like Genesis, it is the seed plot of its revelation. The Seed of The Virgin shall come, the Desired of all nations, and shall be born of God and have two natures. But when he appears, he shall be despised and rejected of men. He will agree to be smitten unto death by heaven, that others may live, and will yield up his life on a cross. He will return thereafter, in vengeful wrath to destroy his enemies, and reap an awful harvest of doom.

2. **Summary of the House of LIBRA**—The Scales demand a debt payment that no one can make, but that shall be made by the

death of a Victim upon a Cross, at the hands of a Person with Two Natures, and the Victim immediately receives a Crown. An incredibly precise summary of the Atoning work of Christ!

3. **Summary of the House of SCORPIO**—The Scorpion is the Great Enemy of the Seed of the Woman, the Serpent, and shall bruise His heel even as the Man bruises his head. The struggle between the two is for dominion, and the Serpent seeks to wear the crown, but is prevented by the Man, who overcomes him in great struggle. The Man, the Strong One Who Cometh, shall bruise the Serpent's head. A precise summary of the struggle between Christ and Satan.

4. **Summary of the House of SAGITTARIUS**—The two-natured archer, a centaur identical to the one making the sacrifice over the Cross, shall triumph gloriously over his foes, and shall be greatly praised by those that he delivers. He shall finish the judgement against the Great Serpent and his allies, and bring wrath and a great curse upon them to the uttermost.

THE SECOND BOOK—
THE REDEEMED, BLESSINGS PROCURED

5. **Summary of the House of CAPRICORNUS**—The dying sacrificial Goat, struck by the arrow of judgement, is the same with the dying Eagle. This sacrificial death is the "wounding in the heel" suffered by the Seed of the Woman in the great struggle with the Serpent. Out of this death will come the resurrection of the Sacrifice and the life of The Rest of Her Seed.

6. **Summary of the House of AQUARIUS**—The Redeemer shall pour out a river of blessing upon the Redeemed, then He shall go away to a Far Place; but He shall Return surely and swiftly to Judge His Enemies and Reward His Redeemed.

7. **Summary of the House of PISCES**—The bound Fishes and the Chained Woman are one and the same, bound to the great monster, but freed by the Redeemer, the Seed of the Woman, Who shall bruise the Serpent's head, then rule as King over all.

8. **Summary of the House of ARIES**—The Redeemer, though bruised in the effort, shall interdict the Sea Monster's binding power and free the Woman, and then elevate her to a heavenly throne beside the King. In so doing, He shall bruise the Monster's head and bind him with chains.

THE THIRD BOOK—
THE REDEEMER, <u>HIS 2ND COMING</u>

9. **Summary of the House of TAURUS**—The Saviour, who was wounded and slain, shall come as a great Bull, bearing his congregation upon his shoulders, and goring his enemies in judgement. The Branch of the Woman shall triumph over his great Enemy like a mighty hunter, shining with glorious light, and trampling the enemy's Head and destroying it. He shall send forth a River of terrible judgement. Like a tender Shepherd, he will gather his Flock in his arms and protect them.

10. **Summary of the House of GEMINI**—The Branch, The Seed of The Woman, He Who has two natures, shall come as both a suffering Redeemer and a triumphant Judge, and he shall bruise the head of the enemy.

11. **Summary of the House of CANCER**—The meaning of Cancer and its decans is that there is One Who treads upon the Serpent's Head and holds a great multitude of Redeemed Ones in safety in His hands. This multitude is composed of Two Flocks, one latter in time and much greater in size than the earlier. They will ultimately travel together in great safety, as in a ship upon the sea.

12. **Summary of the House of LEO**—The Great Lion, Who is the Seed of the Woman, Coming in Judgement, shall crush the head of His old Enemy the Serpent, and utterly destroy him, pouring upon him wrath and fury to the uttermost, and the Raven shall eat the flesh from his dead bones. **And so ends** The Story in The Stars, told by Mazzaroth in His Season.

And the Sweetest Summary of all, in The Words of God Himself, as He told the first installment of The Story in The Stars:

> GEN 3:14-15 And **the LORD God said unto the serpent**, Because thou hast done this, **thou art cursed** above all cattle, and above every beast of the field; upon thy belly shalt thou go, and dust shalt thou eat all the days of thy life: 15 And **I will put <u>enmity</u> between thee and the woman, and between <u>thy seed</u> and <u>her seed</u>; it shall bruise thy head, and thou shalt bruise his heel.**

And so THAT STORY WAS TOLD by the Patriarchs, for over 2500 years...'til God passed it to Moses, and told him to start WRITING DOWN THE THE WORDS.

'Twas With An Everlasting Love

'Twas with an everlasting love, [The Woman's Seed His Bride embraced],
Before [God] made the worlds above, or Earth on her huge columns placed.

Long ere the Sun's refulgent ray Primeval Shades of Darkness drove
[She] on His Sacred Bosom lay, loved with an Everlasting Love.

Then, in His Love and [God's] decrees, [Bridegroom and] Bride appeared as one;
Her sin, by imputation His, while She in spotless splendor shone.

O Love! How high thy glory swell! How great, immutable, and free;
Ten thousand sins as black as Hell, are swallowed up, O Love, by Thee.

[Child, IN THE *STARS*] thy Comfort [shines], from First to Last Salvation's free;
[God's] Everlasting Love [doth tell, That] Everlasting [Story *SEEN*].

> John Kent (1766-1843, 77 yrs)
> [alterations mine COJ]

*****

Chapter 4—
The Amazing Credibility Gap

Before we get amazed, let's be sure we understand the meanings of some key words.

> **credibility.** noun. The quality of being trusted and <u>believed in</u>: *the government's loss of credibility.*
> - the quality of being convincing or <u>believable</u>: *the book's anecdotes have scant regard for credibility.*
>
> Etymology: mid 16th century, from Latin *credibilitas*, from *credibilis* (see "credible").
>
> **credible.** adj. Able to be <u>believed</u>; convincing: *few people found his story credible | a credible witness.*
> - capable of persuading people that something will happen or be successful: *a credible threat.*
>
> Etymology: late Middle English, from Latin *credibilis*, from *credere* 'believe.'
>
> **credibility gap.** noun. An apparent difference between what is said or promised and what happens or is true.
>
> [all Oxford American, my emphases COJ]

The specific Credibility Gap we are considering is Something that was once believed, but is now rejected, *even though it actually happened and is now seen to be True.*

The amazing thing is SOME of the People whose ancient history shows they *used* to believe The Story in the Stars; but *now* that two thirds of it have happened and proven True, they *no longer believe it!* Isn't that amazing? Believed it Foretold for thousands of years, then when it came True—*exactly* as foretold—*rejected it!*

And who are These People, who once believed and now reject, The Story in the Stars? The Jews, The Arabic Peoples, and the Scientists, specifically the Astronomers...these are the ones who most interest us. Why? For a most amazing reason: their Progenitors are *the very ones* who wrote down millennia ago, then passed on down to us, The Story in the Stars, Mazzaroth in his seasons.

The Jews

The progenitors of the Jews descended from Noah's son Shem (father of the Semites), down through Eber (a Semite, and father of the Hebrews), and finally to Abram, renamed by God as Abraham (a Semite and a Hebrew). God promised Abraham would be the Father of Many Nations. One of Abraham's sons was Isaac (a Semite and a Hebrew, like his father). One of Isaac's sons was Jacob, God renamed him Israel (thus a Semite, a Hebrew, and father of the Israelites). Finally, one of Jacob's 12 sons was Judah (a Semite, a Hebrew, an Israelite, and thus finally father of the Jews). These distinctions were quite important in ancient times (not all Semites were Hebrews, not all Hebrews were Israelites, and not all Israelites were Jews...even though all Jews were Israelites, Hebrews, and Semites). But during Jeremiah's ministry, God told him

> Jer 34:9 That every man should let his manservant, and every man his maidservant, being an **Hebrew** or an **Hebrewess**, go free; that none should serve himself of them, **to wit, of a Jew his brother**.

From this time forward (~588 BC)—although *specific* distinctions remained important, and remembered—the terms Hebrew, Israelite, and Jew meant the same thing, for all *practical* purposes. So, with very little tongue in cheek, and no *practical* error at all, one may call Abraham the First *Theological* Jew—one who (regardless of their biology) professes faith in the Theology of the Jews, and converts by circumcision. Although not *biologically* Jewish (tho' he was a Semite and a Hebrew) he became *nevertheless*, as shown, the biological progenitor of the Jews.

It is very important to pay attention to exactly what God *says*, because that is exactly what God *means*—Grammatical/literalism is the Bible's own hermeneutic. So, do you see what this all comes down to? A theological Jew, who was not a biological Jew, became the progenitor of all biological Jews, some of whom apostatize and are no longer theological Jews. See? I thought that might clear things up some. Just read a King James Bible (some of the revised 'bibles' have changed some key words, and screwed all this up to hell and gone).

Why is this important? The progenitors of the Jewish People, from Adam to Abraham, and the Jewish People from Abraham to Christ, all believed the Story in the Stars told by Mazzaroth in his seasons. They maintained both the integrity and antiquity of the Zodiac from the time of the Ark of Noah, with more than sufficient evidence to repudiate the fatuous pretensions of Astrology and the Astrological Zodiac to historical originality. In fact, as I have shown, the Hebrew Zodiac contains the oldest names of some of the constellations and stars, *adapted* right into the oldest Sumerian, Egyptian, Indian (via the Parsees), and Arabic Zodiacs. The Jewish historian Josephus relates, for instance, how Abraham taught *Astronomy* (Mazzaroth in his seasons, The Story in the Stars) to the ancient Egyptians (who, of course, knew about Sun, Moon, Stars, and Constellations; but were *Astrologers* at the time).

There is a direct link between certain signs of Mazzaroth and both the Old Testament prophecies concerning the Coming Messiah and the New Testament proclamations of Jesus as being that Christ.

> Isa 7:14 Therefore the Lord himself shall give you a SIGN; **Behold, a <u>virgin</u> shall conceive, and bear a son, and shall call his name Immanuel.** (cp Matt 1:22-23)
>
> John 19:16-18 **Then delivered he** [Pilate] **him** [Jesus] **therefore unto them to be <u>crucified</u>.** And they took Jesus, and led him away. 17 And **he bearing his <u>cross</u>** went forth into a place called the place of a skull, which is called in the Hebrew Golgotha: 18 Where <u>they crucified him</u>...
>
> Gen 49:9-10 **Judah is a lion's whelp**: from the prey, my son, thou art gone up: he stooped down, he couched as a lion, and as an old lion; who shall rouse him up? 10 <u>The sceptre shall not depart from Judah, nor a lawgiver from between his feet,</u> **until Shiloh come**; <u>and unto him shall the gathering of the people be.</u>
>
> —taken together with—
>
> Rev 5:5,9 And one of the elders saith unto me, Weep not: **behold, <u>the Lion of the tribe of Juda</u>, the Root of David**, hath prevailed to open the book, and to loose the seven seals thereof....9 And they sung a new song, saying, <u>Thou art worthy to take the book, and to open the seals thereof: for thou wast slain, and hast redeemed us to God by thy blood out of every kindred, and tongue, and people, and nation</u>...

The prophecy of the Virgin takes us right to the first constellation of Mazzaroth, *Virgo*, a Virgin bearing a Seed in her hand—the very Beginning of The Story in the Stars (see pp. 18-19). Jesus was Crucified—to execute by nailing to a Cross. Continuing through Mazzaroth, we find the constellation *Crux* (the southern cross), *last seen in the horizon of Jerusalem about the time Christ was crucified.* The Old Testament prophesies "They pierced my hands and my feet" (Psa 22:16); and again prophesies that future Israel "shall look upon me whom they have pierced, and they shall mourn for him" (Zec 12:10-11). I have pastored Jewish Christians, who wept like a child when I preached the crucified Christ. The very next constellation in Mazzaroth is *Victima*—The Slain Victim (see pp. 23-24). In the ancient Dendera Egypt Zodiac, this constellation is pictured as a little child with a finger on his lips, named *Sura*, "The Lamb". As it was prophesied in Isa 53:7, "He opened not his mouth," so it was fulfilled at the judgement of Pilate, Jesus "answered him to never a word" (Mtt 27:14). Then, there is the last major constellation of Mazzaroth, *Leo* the Lion. Sure enough, out of the loins of Judah, as was prophesied (Gen 49:9-10), came He Who will throughout eternity be called, The Lion of the tribe of Judah (Rev 5:5,9). And, as I have shown, there are many more such prophetic parallels.

The progenitors of the Jewish People, and the Jewish People themselves, believed The Story in the Stars for over 4000 years—from Creation through the Flood of Noah, down TO the Crucifixion and Resurrection of the Coming One, and His fulfillment of 1500 prophecies in the Old Testament, including 300 Messianic prophecies, *demarking and defining His Identity*, and fulfilling all the promises in the first two Books of the Zodiac...*without a single miss* of promise or prophecy. Then, the Jews did an amazing thing.

They *rejected* Him.

Then, God *rejected* them—His Religion is *no more* any kind of Judaism, save only that which was REFORMED into Christianity, by Jewish Apostles, Jewish prophets, and Jewish Scripture Authors of the New Testament (Heb 9:8-12).

Proof? 70 AD.

The Arabic Peoples

Abraham, at the urging of his wife Sarah, took her Egyptian handmaid as a concubine, and begat a son named Ishmael. Just as did Adam listening to Eve, Abraham listened to Sarah—and generated a hell of a mess, that will bedevil his Jewish Children 'til the last tick of time. Ishmael's Children, you see, are the ancient Arabic Peoples.

Ishmael (Who, as his father, *was* a Semite and a Hebrew, but *not* an Israelite—they came from his half-brother Isaac through his son Jacob) became the father of the Ishmaelites, who then produced the Arabic Peoples (who, for all practical purposes, are as Semitic and Hebrew as any Jew). Any Arab who denies he is a Hebrew denies his Abrahamic lineage. All of this can lead to interesting conundrums. If an Arabic Hebrew (member of Hamas) and a Jewish Hebrew (Israeli soldier) fight to the death (in Gaza), are they *both* anti-Semites? *Why not?* As I said, a hell of a mess. Sorta reminds you of Cain and Abel, doesn't it?

Modern DNA studies are fascinating, the way they confirm much of these ancient family records, both Jewish and Arabic, preserved in the Old Testament. The Jewish word *Cohen* ("priest") points to Jews with that last name. Over 50% of them, world over, bear a marker in their DNA now called the Cohen marker, which identifies them as descending from the old Jewish priesthood, and thus identifies them coming from the tribe of Levi, the tribe of priests, tracing back to around 1500-1400 BC, at the time of the Exodus (to Aaron, Moses' brother). Logically, this *implies* that markers that *could* identify the other 11 tribes must *still* exist, or the Cohen marker otherwise could not—we just have no way now to identify the others.

But, it gets better. DNA markers *must* have antecedents. When we trace backward in time carefully, generation by generation back from Aaron, then back past Levi, we come to a DNA Progenitor of the Cohen marker, a direct ancestor of Levi, with a truly astounding characteristic—He can be shown, beyond refutation, to be the genetic Father of Several Nations, *including both the Jews and the Arabic Peoples!* There is no known individual in history, fitting these characteristics more genetically or logically, than the Biblical Abraham, Father of Many Nations! The Story in the Stars and the text of the Masoretic Hebrew Old Testament, the Ancestral Faith of the Jews and the Arabic Peoples, is thus logically and scientifically confirmed in part by the science of DNA. I highly recommend the book **DNA & Tradition, the Genetic Link to the Ancient Hebrews,** by Rabbi Yaakov Kleiman.

Thus we can identify the Progenitors of *both* the Jews and the Arabic Peoples—one and the same, Abraham and his progenitors—all the way back to Shem and his father Noah...and thru them and the preceding Patriarchs, who told The Story in the Stars (of One Coming through the Bloodline), all the way back to Adam and Eve.

Let us make *one precise distinction*. I do this relying upon the authenticity of the oldest and purest Hebrew text, the Masoretic, which underlies the King James Bible Old Testament. Ancient copies of the Masoretic Text were found in the caves of the Dead Sea Scrolls, dating from 50-250 BC. Until then, the oldest Masoretic text we had was the Aleppo Codex dated ~950 AD. When these texts, separated by over 1000 years were compared, they were found to be virtually the same (save for spelling differences, some word order, and some marginal notes). The historical authenticity of the Masoretic Text, in its purest copies, cannot be successfully gainsaid. The most conservative Jewish scholars often refer to it as, "The old original Hebrew."

That is the only Hebrew Text I accept as Scripture. The King James Old Testament was translated *exclusively* from *that* Text.

Now, what's the *precise distinction* I wish to make? Here it is,

> Gen 17:18 And Abraham said unto God, O that Ishmael might live before thee! 19 **And God said**...20 And as for Ishmael, I have heard thee: Behold, I have blessed him, and will make him fruitful, and will multiply him exceedingly; twelve princes shall he beget, and I will make him a great nation. 21 **But my covenant will I establish with Isaac**...22 And he left off talking with him, and God went up from Abraham.

The most ancient and demonstrably error-free Hebrew text, the Masoretic, declares *unmistakably* that "**God said**...My covenant will I establish with Isaac." Make no mistake...the descent of the Chosen Bloodline through Isaac, *not Ishmael*, was a Decree of the God of Abraham. Any babbling yap whatsoever that says the Jews changed the text to read that way is simply a load of lying crapola *that cannot be proven* from any amount of historical or manuscript evidence.

Can I *prove* that?

No, I simply *believe* that. BUT...*Why* am I willing to believe *that*?

Three good reasons that *can* be proven. **1st**, No confirmative manuscript evidence exists that proves God *didn't* say it, just as the Masoretic text describes (and it incorporates over 82% of the very best manuscript evidence). **2nd**, Archaeological evidence and Mathematical Probability establish as *both valid and true* the statements of the King James English (and the underlying Masoretic Hebrew and Textus Receptus Greek texts)—see Appendix 1, The Bible Validated. **3rd**, I *believe* it because the *validated* King James Bible (thus the *validated* Masoretic Hebrew) *says* it.

Be careful of *any* lying crapola that tells you we don't have a verbally and plenarily inspired, inerrant, Scripture, given and preserved by God, for the use of His People. There is ONE. But, there are also *Many* corrupt and pretentious books that *aren't. And DON'T forget the DNA Cohen Marker—IT COMES DOWN FROM ISAAC, NOT ISHMAEL!*

The Arabic Peoples received Mazzaroth in his seasons, The Story in the Stars, from their father Ishmael; who was taught it as a child, in the tent of his father Abraham. As shown by their Zodiacs, with relatively little variation from that of the Jews, the Arabic Peoples looked for the dual-natured Coming One Who would battle the Serpent for His Bride. Then, Christ came, was Crucified and Resurrected, then ascended back to Heaven—thus fulfilling all the promises of

The Story in the Stars, and 1500 prophecies of the Hebrew Scripture, *without a single miss* in either. Then, the Arabic Peoples did an amazing thing.

They *rejected* Him...mainly, because He did not descend from Ishmael.

Then, for almost 600 years, they gradually relinquished Mazzaroth in his season, and slipped away into the ancient Sumerian Astrological Zodiac, held by most infidels. Then in 610, Mohammed, believed to be a direct descendant from Ishmael, preached the first message of the Holy Koran, which would become accepted as Holy Scripture by most of the Arabic Peoples (and in later years, many others). With no disrespect intended, I use the word "Koran", because that is the familiar English translation of the Arabic word "*Qur'an*" ("recitation"), and I am an English writer and speaker. The Holy Koran complete, contains 114 chapters, called *Suras* in Arabic, each with varying numbers of what may be called Verses, similar to Jewish and Christian Bibles.

There are A NUMBER OF FACTS...such as this *rejection*...about both Mohammed and the Holy Koran, THAT ARE *CONFUSING*, to non-Muslims.

Take Mohammed. All Muslims profess and believe that he is the Greatest Prophet. They all confess that Jesus Christ is also a great prophet, but they believe that Mohammed is the *Greatest* Prophet, greater than Christ, and greater than all the Jewish prophets that went before, and greater than all the New Testament prophets that came after. That is not confusing—that is a clear article of faith. Here is what is confusing—*WHY* is Mohammed a *greater* prophet? Christ and the other Biblical prophets together made over 1800 prophecies, 1500 of which *have come to pass, without a single miss!* Mohammed, throughout his entire life, *did not make one single Bible-type prophecy.* He did make about 22 near-term predictions, concerning various battles and ongoing events, but that is *not* a Bible-type prophecy. Bible-type prophecies involve decades, centuries, even millennia time spans, and include specific names, events, and outcomes. What is *confusing* to non-Muslims is, "Which is *Greater*, 1500 or...*ZERO*?

Much the same confusion involves the Holy Koran itself. The Holy Bible contains 1800 prophecies, over 1500 of which have been fulfilled *without a single miss* (consider the mathematical probability of that happening by chance—see Appendix 1, The Bible Validated, the Proof from Prophecy). In fact, over 25% of The Bible is dealing with prophecy. But...the Holy Koran *does not contain even one Bible-*

type prophecy...1800 vs. ZERO! What's with *that*? The God of Abraham said,

> Isa 46:9-11 **Remember the former things of old: for I am God, and there is none else; I am God, and there is none like me**, **10 Declaring the end from the beginning, and from ancient times the things that are not yet done**, saying, My counsel shall stand, and I will do all my pleasure: 11 Calling a ravenous bird from the east, the man that executeth my counsel from a far country: **yea, I have spoken it, I will also bring it to pass; I have purposed it, I will also do it.**

Then, He did it...so far, *1500 times without a single miss*. The God of Abraham does this in The Holy Bible to prove, "There is none else, there is none like me." God does this to prove that NOBODY ELSE CAN DO IT. But then, in the Holy Koran, Allah (whom Mohammed tells us *is* the God of Abraham) neither so proves himself, nor proves his greatest prophet, *not even with one* single Bible-type prophecy...*not ever*. Because things that are *Different* are not the *Same*, Non-Muslims find this...*CONFUSING*.

Another *confusing* fact to non-Muslims is the Identity of *Allah*. From 610 (the first preaching of Mohammed) until now, there is not the slightest confusion about Mohammed proclaiming that Allah is the God of Abraham. The confusion among non-Muslims is, Who was the god named *Allah* BEFORE Mohammed started preaching? This is important because, in all of human history, only One God was ever named *Yehovah Elohim*—the God of Abraham (and He says THAT is His *memorial Name* forever, see Exo 3:14-15).

Before Mohammed came, for over a thousand years, some of the Arabic Peoples indeed worshipped a god called *Allah*. But, what is *confusing* to non-Muslims is that he was the moon god, whose symbol was the crescent moon, and he had three goddess daughters (*Al-lāt, Manāt* and *al-'Uzzá*). Whoa!...that doesn't fit monotheism. More confusing, the *same* god in nearby regions was called *Sin/Su'en* (with the same crescent moon symbol).

In fact, the name *Sin* (the moon god, symbol the crescent moon) originates in the clay tablets of ancient Sumeria, among the Akkadians (apparently combined by them with the Sumerian god *Nanna*)...a few hundred years after the Tower of Babel (back around 2000 BC). The worship of the moon god *Sin* was adopted by the ancient Canaanites, complete with that crescent moon symbol. It became a common practice among ancient *Semitic* peoples to worship that moon god under the name *Allah*. The worship of moon god *Allah*, with his crescent moon symbol, continued down through the centuries among the Semitic peoples, right down into pre-Islamic times in South Arabia. The Quraysh tribe, of which Mohammed was a member, worshipped moon god *Allah* (and his three goddess daughters). Then comes Mohammed, beginning in the year 610, preaching *Allah with a crescent moon symbol*, but now saying he is the God of Abraham. The Holy Koran then says the God of Abraham doesn't have a *Son* (Sura 19:35)—*but, says nothing about those three goddess daughters!* Check "Wikipedia/Sin (mythology), and Muhammed", or any other source on ancient Akkadian mythologies…I'm not making this stuff up. A great many non-Muslims find all this quite…*CONFUSING*.

Another *confusing* thing about the Holy Koran is that it says The Bible is God's Guiding Truth. I will use the M.H. Shakir translation (made for an online version), with my comments in [brackets].

> Sura 5:46-47 And We sent after them in their footsteps **Isa** [Jesus], **son of Marium** [Mary], verifying what was before him of the **Taurat** [Torah] and **We gave him the Injeel** [Gospel] <u>in which was guidance and light</u>, and **verifying what was before it of Taurat** [Law] and <u>a guidance and an admonition</u> for those who guard (against evil). 47 And **the followers of the Injeel** [Gospel] **should have judged by what Allah revealed in it; and** <u>whoever did not judge by what Allah revealed, those are they that are the transgressors.</u>
>
> Sura 10:94 But **if you are in doubt** as to what We have revealed to you, **ask those who read the Book** [The Bible] before you; <u>certainly the truth</u> **has come to you from your Lord, therefore you should not be of the disputers**.

So far, this is not confusing, it is quite clear: Allah (God) says He sent Jesus son of Mary, and gave Him the Gospel, to verify what was in The Law (the Jewish Old Testament). Muslims are told to "ask those who read the Book (The Bible)", and says, "Certainly the truth has come to you from your Lord." Then, Allah says those who do not judge by that revelation "are the transgressors" and "the disputers". To repeat, this is not at all confusing, this is quite clear.

So, what is the *confusing* thing? The confusion results from What Jesus said in the Gospel, while He was verifying what was before in The Law (Jewish Old Testament). When I refer to the Gospel (the New Testament), I accept only the Textus Receptus Greek as Scripture, the oldest and purest of all the early texts. All other texts have been shown to be both *later* than the Textus Receptus and to have dropped, changed, or added words and even books re the Textus Receptus (such as many Roman Catholic manuscripts originating in the

2-4th centuries, and used to translate all the revised versions today). Since the King James New Testament translated the Textus Receptus *exclusively,* that is the only English version I recognize as Scripture. Here, in the King James Bible, is what Jesus said in the Gospel, verifying The Law, that the Holy Koran says is "certainly the truth":

> Exodus 3:14 And **God said** unto Moses, **I AM THAT I AM**: and he said, Thus shalt thou **say unto the children of Israel, I AM hath sent me unto you.**

> John 8:56-59 Your father Abraham rejoiced to see my day: and he saw it, and was glad. 57 Then said the Jews unto him, Thou art not yet fifty years old, and hast thou seen Abraham? 58 **Jesus said unto them**, Verily, verily, I say unto you, BEFORE ABRAHAM WAS, I AM. 59 Then took they up stones to cast at him: but Jesus hid himself, and went out of the temple, going through the midst of them, and so passed by.

—elsewhere in the Gospel (the New Testament) it says—

> Heb 1:1-3a God, who at sundry times and in divers manners spake in time past unto the fathers by the prophets, 2 Hath in these last days spoken unto us by **his Son**, whom he hath appointed heir of all things, by whom also he made the worlds; 3 **Who being** the brightness of his glory, and **the express image of his person**...

> Rom 1:1-4 Paul, a servant of Jesus Christ, called to be an apostle, separated unto **the gospel of God**, 2 (Which he had promised afore by his prophets in the holy scriptures,) 3 **Concerning his Son Jesus Christ our Lord**, which was made of the seed of David according to the flesh; 4 And **declared to be the Son of God with power**, according to the spirit of holiness, by the resurrection from the dead:

> 1 John 5:20 And we know that the Son of God is come, and hath given us an understanding, that we may know him that is true, and we are in him that is true, even in **his Son** Jesus Christ. **This is the true God**, and eternal life.

Jesus Christ, verifying The Law (Old Testament), identified His *Divine* Nature as I AM. The Gospel (New Testament) says that Jesus Christ was the Son of God AND that His Son Jesus Christ is the True God...AND the True God, the God of Abraham, calls Himself I AM.

The Holy Koran tells us what Jesus taught in the Gospel was Truth. And IN the Gospel, Jesus Christ identifies *His Divine Nature* (not his human nature) as I AM, the God of Abraham. The Gospel also tells us that Jesus Christ is "the true God, and eternal life." Thus,

The Bible shows how Christ was dual-natured—*just like the Seed of the Woman in the Zodiac.* BUT THEN...Mohammed and the Holy Koran *reject* Jesus Christ as *both* the God of Abraham (Divine Nature) and the Son of God (human nature). Because things that are *Different* are not the *Same,* do you see how...CONFUSING...all of this is, to non-Muslims?

VERY IMPORTANT *CONFUSIONS* SUMMARIZED

1. The Moon God *Sin/Su'en*, with a crescent moon symbol, appeared among the pagans around 2000 BC, after the Tower of Babel. When Ishmael's children began to multiply (after about 1700-1600 BC), they worshipped the Moon God, with a crescent moon symbol, and began to call him *Allah*. Some hundreds of years later, they began to also worship his three goddess daughters (*Allāt, Manāt,* and *al-'Uzzá*)—right down to 609 AD, *the year BEFORE* Mohammed began to preach.

2. Mohammed tells us in the Holy Koran, that The Bible is God's Guiding Truth. Therein, Allah says He sent Jesus son of Mary, and gave Him the Gospel, to verify what was in The Law (the Jewish Old Testament). In The Law, The God of Abraham calls Himself I AM. In the Gospel, Jesus identifies His *divine* nature as I AM, and His *human* nature is called The Son of God with Power. In The Law (Deut 32:16-17) and in The Gospel (1 Cor 10:19-22), God's Guiding Truth tells us that *ALL* FALSE GODS COME FROM SATAN.

3. Then, beginning after 610, Mohammed in the Holy Koran *denies* that Jesus is God; and then he begins to deny that Jesus is any son of God at all, saying that Allah has no son; and finally, he ceases to mention Allah the Moon God's three goddess daughters he had worshipped all his life (they sort of fade away quietly), *although the 2600 year old crescent moon symbol was retained.*

4. In The Law (Dan 10:16; 9:21-23), the angel Gabriel appears to the prophet Daniel. He speaks very gently and respectfully to him, and tells him he is "greatly beloved." He then explains a very detailed vision sent by God. In The Gospel (Luke 1:19-20), Gabriel appears to the prophet Zacharias, husband of Elisabeth (John the Baptist's parents). Though he makes Zacharias mute for his lack of faith, Gabriel is very gentle and respectful. Again in The Gospel (Luke 1:26-38), Gabriel appears to Mary the Mother of Jesus. He speaks extremely respectfully to her and says, "Hail, thou that art highly favoured, the

Lord is with thee: blessed art thou among women....Fear not, Mary: for thou hast found favour with God." He then tells her about the Virgin Birth, saying, "Behold, thou shalt conceive in thy womb, and bring forth a son, and shalt call his name JESUS. He shall be great, and shall be called **the Son of the Highest**." When Mohammed began preaching, he testified that SOMETHING called The Angel Gabriel spoke to him. BUT, when this being spoke to Mohammed, it acted very...*DIFFERENTLY*...from the Angel Gabriel in The Law and in The Gospel. It was blunt and cruel—it upbraided Mohammed, slapped him, beat him, and knocked him to the ground, kicking him.

5. The Muslim civilization produced two of the finest philosophers of the Middle Ages, Avicenna (980–1037, 57 yrs) and Averroes (c.1126–98, 72 yrs). They were consummate Logicians. They both understood *perfectly well* and taught the Primary Laws of all Thought, especially The First Law of Thought, upon which *all* else is based— The Principle of Contradiction, A ≠ non-A, or:

Things that are DIFFERENT **are *NOT* the Same.**

Do you see how...*CONFUSING*...all of this is, to non-Muslims? WHY are things in the Holy Koran so...*DIFFERENT*...from The Taurat and The Injeel? *Both* of which the Holy Koran says are "guidance and light".

As I said—as shown by their Zodiacs, with relatively little variation from that of the Jews, the Arabic Peoples looked for the Coming One, the dual-natured Seed of The Woman, Who would battle the Serpent for His Bride. Then, Christ came, was Crucified and Resurrected, then ascended back to Heaven—thus fulfilling all the promises of The Story in the Stars found in the first two books of the Zodiac, and also 1500 prophecies of the Hebrew Scripture, *without a single miss* in either. Then, just as did the Jews, the Arabic Peoples did an amazing thing...

They *rejected* Him...mainly, because He did not descend from Ishmael...even though the God of Abraham said in The Law [Taurat], "My covenant will I establish with Isaac," (Gen 17:21).

The Scientists (primarily Astronomers)

Let's start this one off on the right foot, and make sure that foot is planted upon solid ground.

astronomy. Noun the branch of <u>science</u> that deals with celestial objects, space, and the physical universe as a whole.

<u>In ancient times, observation of the sun, moon, stars, and planets formed the basis of timekeeping and navigation.</u> Astronomy was greatly furthered by the invention of the optical telescope, but modern observations are made in all parts of the spectrum, including X-ray and radio frequencies, using terrestrial and orbiting instruments and space probes.

[Oxford American, my emphasis COJ]

astrology. Noun the study of the movements and relative positions of celestial bodies *<u>interpreted as having</u> <u>an influence on human affairs and the natural world</u>*.

Ancient observers of the heavens developed <u>elaborate systems of explanation</u> based on the movements of the sun, moon, and planets through the constellations of the zodiac, <u>for predicting events and for casting horoscopes. By 1700 astrology had lost intellectual credibility in the West</u>, but continued to have popular appeal. Modern astrology is based on that of the Greeks, but other systems are extant, notably those of China and India.

[Oxford American, my emphasis COJ]

Notice, under the right foot, we have "science"; but under the left foot we have "dum-dum doo-doo" (technical meaning *only*, we are discussing "science", see Glossary...be careful that you have a rubber boot on that left foot). Let us stand for a while on the *right* foot.

In ancient times, developing accurate timekeeping and navigation required *rigorous* mathematical measurements of those celestial objects and their movements, and mathematics is the *essential* language of science. Thus, when discussing Astronomy, we are discussing a science. When did it first start? 24 Sept 4004 BC, evening of the 4th Day, when God created the stars *and gave them their names* (Gen 1:14-19; Psa 147:4; see p.1 ¶2).

But, when using Astrology, we must imagine something "interpreted as having", and then dream up "elaborate systems of explanation...for predicting events and for casting horoscopes". Thus, when discussing Astrology, we are discussing dum-dum doo-doo (technical meaning *only*). When did *that* first start? About 3769 BC (~235 years *after* the science of Astronomy began), when men began to *profane* The Story in the Stars, by *changing* The Story in The Stars, from the *religious* purpose that God intended, into something...*Different* (see p. 11).

About 1421 years after *profaning* The Story in the Stars began, God destroyed the Old World in 2348 BC, with what we call The Flood of Noah. Human civilization as we know it thus began anew, about 4366 years ago (writing this in 2018). In our most ancient historical records, mainly clay tablets that have been archaeologically recovered, we find that the science of Astronomy, as we have it in the Mazzaroth, was well underway. In those ancient tablets, the Zodiac is attributed to The Creator, as The Bible also says (see pp. 41-42).

Amazingly, in those early records, dating back to ~2300 BC, the science of Astronomy appears full-blown, along with surprisingly advanced mathematics, building construction, and civil engineering technology. No doubt, Noah and his sons brought a lot of that with them, from the Old World, in books on the Ark—the last couple of centuries of that old world seem to have been far more technically advanced than most people realize.

> Ecc 1:9-11 **The thing that hath been, it is that which shall be**; and that which is done is that which shall be done: and **there is no new thing under the sun. 10 Is there any thing whereof it may be said, See, this is new? it hath been already of old time, which was before us.** 11 There is no remembrance of former things; neither shall there be any remembrance of things that are to come with those that shall come after.

Read that passage carefully, then remember that God *told* Solomon to write those words down—*Solomon did* NOT *dream them up with creative imagination* (2 Pet 1:21). You see, God knows what that old world was like before it ended, and He knows what our present world will be like before it ends (in the not too distant future—remember, Israel has Returned to the Land and we are now in what Christ called the Last Generation, Luke 21:23-24, 31-33). So, when God tells Solomon "There is no new thing under the sun...It hath *already been* of old time, *which was before us*," then that is a *fact*, not a metaphor. Would you say that space ships to the Moon, nuclear bombs, and genetic engineering are "new"? Then what about, "It hath been already of old time"? Are you *sure* those things were not around in the Old World? Were *You* there? GOD WAS.

See?

So, from the beginning of our present world, over 4300 years ago, Scientists have believed surprisingly accurate versions of Mazzaroth in his seasons, The Story in the Stars...*according to their own surviving clay tablet records*. Even as The Story degraded, due to the pervasive influence of dum-dum doo-doo Astrology (not to mention the confusion of tongues at the Tower of Babel), many of the names of the constellations survived, along with the original names of their brightest stars, carrying important pieces of The Story in the Stars, right down to the Time of Christ...all around the world...and many of those ancient Scientists believed it.

Then, Christ was born. In His brief lifetime, He fulfilled all the prophetic aspects of the first two books of Mazzaroth, as well as 1500 Old Testament prophecies, including 300 of them *specifying His exact Identity...all without missing a single one.* Then all the Scientists who had believed part or all of The Story in the Stars did an amazing thing.

They *rejected* Him.

Over the next century or so, every fragment of The Story in the Stars, all around the world, was dropped by those Scientists; and they increasingly embraced the fairy tale that Astrology, and fortune telling, was all the Zodiac ever portended...*despite the evidence in clay tablets and ancient writings to the contrary.*

Modern Scientists embrace that Astrology fairy tale, and teach it at fine universities like Harvard, using poo-bah **P**iled **h**igh and **D**eep, so that it seems...*Plausibly Credible.*

First, they laughingly point out that stars are far away, some of them millions of light years away, so the Genesis 7-day Creation story can't be true...it would have taken millions of years for the starlight to reach earth, so the stars couldn't have been seen in the Beginning. Bible Believers simply point to Gen 1:3, "Let there be light"; and then read vss. 14-19 when the stars were created, and point out, "Let them be for lights in the firmament of the heaven to give light upon the earth: *and it was so*"; and then conclude that God *created the beams of intervening starlight as well as the stars.* Thus, using light speed to date the universe as millions of years old is a logical fallacy, merely dum-dum doo-doo **P**iled **h**igh and **D**eep (millions and billions deep).

Then the Scientists say, "We've got Radiometric Dating, and we can show mathematically that it takes millions of years for many parent elements to radioactively decay into daughter elements, so the 7-day Creation Story is wrong." Bible Believers point out that ground water leaching invalidates that. Scientists say, "Huh?" Bible Believers explain that ground water in the soil, washing back and forth for years, would leach away any parent/daughter evidence of intervening decay, rendering impossible any dating method of that sort. They also point out that the most resistant substance known, to ground water leaching, is volcanic glass; and that less than a fraction of 1% of radioactive elements found in nature are embedded in volcanic glass; and since even that is permeable to ground water leaching, at a threshold of 30,000 years, therefore it is *impossible* to use radioactive dating on any radioactive materials found in the earth to date anything beyond 30,000 years—so, any radiometric dating beyond that limit is a fallacy. Finally, they point out that 30,000 years is over 33 orders of magnitude *closer* to 6,000 years than even the *first* million years (let alone *billions*). Scientists stare back, unblinking (like fish on ice).

Back when I was pastoring a Baptist Church in Las Vegas, I was invited to give a luncheon talk to a professional engineering society. I explained about 6 Day Creation and the fallacies of various modern dating methods. I thought that might be interesting to scientists and engineers. I wound up explaining the fallacy of radiometric dating, as I did here. When I finished, I opened the floor for any questions. There were about 3 dozen engineers and scientists in the audience with bachelor degrees, about 15 or so with masters, and almost a dozen Ph.D.s. There was not one single response...*not one*...just silence (you coulda heard a cricket, 'cept the Vegas heat had killed 'em all). I thanked them, sat down, and we had a delicious lunch—they do gots great food in Vegas! I was told by the engineer who invited me, that at the next business meeting, the society voted to never invite another speaker unless they had a science or engineering degree from an accredited college or university. Now, I have a Business degree from Auburn University, and half an MBA from the University of Alabama, both nationally-known accredited *science* schools. But, you see, I myself am an ignoramus...I ain't got no science or engineering degree, only a Business degree, with a double concentration in Economics and Information Technology (one o' them there computer-thingies). Still, I consider their response to my talk to be one of the highest professional compliments I have ever been paid.

Some scientists respond, "Wait! We don't need radiometric dating from the ground...we've got Carbon-14, and it's up in the air! So, 6 Day Creation won't work." Bible Believers respond that it takes about 30,000 years to stabilize the C-14 cycle, from start to finish; and that the latest measurements indicate the cycle is only about 22,000 years along, at the most. Furthermore, if you adjust for a cloud cover around the earth, so we can have jungles at the north and south poles (that we have actually found there, under the ice), then the amount of C-14 in the air would indicate an atmospheric age of less than 10,000 years...very close to the Biblically indicated date of a 6-Day Creation a little over 6,000 years ago. The scientists give you that blank-eyed fish-stare again.

Then they respond, "Aw, Evolution refutes all of that Bibley stuff. The universe evolved by Big-Banging into existence out of nothing, and then over billions of years, life finally evolved out of dead things into all the live stuff there is. All of nature will continue evolving like this billions more years, so 6-Day Creation can't be true."

There is a lot of assumption in that gumption (look the definitions up, I'm using the words in a quite literal sense). **First**—a lot of scientists from fine schools like Harvard do believe THAT the universe Big-Banged into existence out of nothing...BUT...none of them have ever been able to explain HOW it happened. Exactly HOW does Nothing 'bang'?

> **nothing.** Pronoun not anything; no single thing.
> • (in calculations) no amount; zero.
>
> **bang.** A sudden loud noise.
> • a sharp blow causing a sudden loud noise.
>
> [Oxford American]

Exactly HOW does no amount of anything go bang? No scientist, from even the finest schools, has ever been able to demonstrate or explain that.

"Not so," some scientists say, "There are scientists who have shown, with advanced mathematics, how such a thing *might* happen." Bible Believers point out, that won't work. You see, some Mathematicians have the fallacious belief that if you can describe something mathematically, and if the mathematics are *valid*, that means the mathematics are *true*. Why is that fallacious? Because you are talking about two *different* things. Looky here,

> **valid.** Adj. (of an argument or point) having a sound basis in logic or fact; reasonable or cogent.
>
> [Oxford American, my emphasis]
>
> **true.** The way things actually are. [Philosophical def.]

Mathematics is a subset of Verbal Language (Proof: No aspect of mathematics has any meaning until defined by verbal language). In school, did they teach you words with numbers, or did they teach you numbers *with words*? See? To make a *proper* statement in words, you must use *correct grammar*, but it might be true or false. Likewise, you can make an improper statement in words using bad grammar, but still it might be true or false. Example:

> All blue cows lay green eggs—Grammatically correct, but not true (there are no blue cows, cows don't lay eggs).
>
> Ain't nobody can baptize no tiger—Grammatically incorrect, but true (grab one by the neck and try).

You see, mathematical *validity* is the same as verbal *grammar*, but neither one *necessarily* has anything to do with *True*, which is The way things actually are. And therein lies the fallacious foible which underlies so much Modern Scientific Theory, making it seem so... *Plausibly Credible*. Especially when taught as true, at fine schools like Harvard. Here's the gimmick—Many scientists *fallaciously* assert that if a mathematical equation (or a set of them, called a model) is mathematically *Valid*, then it must be *True*, as if Valid and True were the same thing, *but they are not*. That gimmick, that fallacious foible, I define as *Mathemagic* (see Glossary)—if people don't know what is being done, then a scientist can use mathemagic to make poot stink in the wind smell like roses...*lotsa* roses, **P**iled **h**igh and **D**eep.

So...*exactly* How...did the universe bang into existence *out of Nothing*? No scientist can tell you...*without using Mathemagic*. But...THAT it happened...so many scientists fervently believe. To *imagine* that it happened, then to write down those dreams in *Valid* mathemagical equations, does not make them *True*; any more than writing down dreams with *Correct Grammar* makes a fairy tale true.

>For instance: "Once upon a time, in a non-existential moment far, far away, *AbsolutelyNothing* suddenly went... POOOT! (without any bummy hole at all)...and *there* was the Universe!"

Will they let you teach That at Harvard? Certainly not. But, **if** the Scientists retell *the exact same concepts*, but instead use *Valid* mathematical equations and models, **then** they are allowed to teach *That* drivel at Harvard and other fine schools...*every single day*. Please go to the Glossary and look up the term "Dum-dum Doo-doo". Do you perceive any...*Cognitive Relevance*? Thank you. You might also want to go back to the Glossary and look up "Brainwashing". *Whoa!*—why are you running around, and laughing and laughing and laughing?

Second, another assumption in the gumption—How do live things *evolve* from dead things? The scientists say, "Tiny changes, over millions of years." Really? All things, dead things and live things, are made up of various combinations of about 94 types of atoms that occur in Nature. But live things have one thing that dead things *never ever* have. DNA (look it up, I don't want to do all the typing—No, really, look it up...there's a lot of good info, if you're using an Apple Computer dictionary). A strand of DNA is like a small library. DNA is composed of 4 basic parts, like letters of an alphabet. They combine to make larger parts like words. Those are strung together in even larger parts like sentences. And *those* parts are strung together to make finished strands like books...*lotsa* books. Arizona State University has a neat website called Ask A Biologist (https://askabiologist.asu.edu). Under "DNA ABCs", the author writes, "The full set of instructions is so long that it would take more than 3,000 books to print it out. Each book would have 1,000 pages and each page 1,000 letters. To read these instructions would take more than nine years." That's the DNA complexity in even the simplest *living* one cell animal or plant or analogous doohickey. Not only does DNA describe and determine how every living thing is made, but also *how it functions*. *Every* function *capable* to a living thing is coded in its DNA—if it ain't in there, it don't never get done, no how...that's just the way it is.

So...HOW do the scientists tell us, that live things *evolve* from dead things? "Tiny changes, over millions of years." Without DNA, *there is no life...actual* or *possible*. Where does the DNA come from? "Tiny changes, over millions of years." Yeah? *Really?* Changes in *exactly* WHAT? There are only two possibilities—changes in *dead* things or changes in *live* things. *Nothing* is in a dead thing except...well, *dead* things. There are *no* live things to change, **so that option is out**. So, in a dead thing, nothing can change but dead things, and then you will still have a dead thing. Let's make lots of tiny changes, over millions of years. Whatcha got? Dead things—that's all we ever had, that's all we ever did, so that's all we ever got. The Scientists say, "But you are forgetting that all those tiny changes gradually added up to life." To which a Bible Believer responds by slapping the table loudly, jumping up, and *shouting*, "Changes in...*exactly*...WHAT?" That is what no scientist anywhere has any idea how to answer. They simply repeat, like a religious mantra, "Tiny changes, over millions of years," then wiggle their fingers in your face and chant, "Pee Aitch Dee!" (as if that meant something). To people that actually read King James Bibles (and the underlying Hebrew and Greek), *that don't mean squat*. If we grant that tiny changes over millions of years produce life, then it is absolutely true that...*AT SOME POINT*... 'dead' changes to 'live'—so, Mr. Ph.D., lean over the facts-table and put your pointing finger on...*exactly...that...point*. None can do it. Why not? Because in order for *any* life to exist *at all*, then...*AT THAT POINT*... there must *instantly* appear 3,000 books, with a 1,000 pages each, and a 1,000 letters per page of DNA instructions...OR THERE AIN'T NO LIFE, NO HOW, DR. KNUCKLEHEAD, Ph.D.! If he claims they *do* appear *anyway*, then the Bible Believer slaps the table and shouts again, "Changes in...*exactly*...WHAT?...*exactly*...HOW?" And 100 Ph.D.s, from 100 fine schools like Harvard, just frown back...*without a sound*. **And so dies the only other option.**

Some Scientists attempt a feeble comeback, and insist that Charles Darwin solved the problem, starting with *living* things anyway. They insist it was done by Natural Selection and Survival of the Fittest. G. Ledyard Stebbins, one of the formulators of the Neo-Darwinian Theory (they had to reinvent it in the early 20th century, because all Darwin's original assumptions had failed by then), estimated that it required about 500 small selective steps of variation to produce a new species. That would be about 500 missing links between each species. A scientist on the British Museum website opined that there were "hundreds of thousands" of terminal species, many of them found in fossil form, and lying in the museums around the world. To keep it conservative, let's use just 200,000 (I know, many would insist upon much more, *but* I'm trying to be nice). Now, 500 missing links x 200,000 terminal species = at least 100 million missing links total. Darwin himself is known to have told friends, that if all the missing links remained missing, it would be *the strongest refutation* of his theory of Evolution. OK then, How many of those missing links, that Darwin and the evolutionists admit *must* have existed, have *actually* been found, and are lying in museums beside the terminal species fossils they *supposedly* produced? Remember what *True* means—the way things *actually are*. Well, the way things actually are is—ALL THE MISSING LINKS ARE MISSING...*every*...*single*...*one*. Last Question: Is Evolution *really* true, or is it *just* dum-dum doo-doo (technical meaning only, we are discussing Biology and Mathematical Probability)?

Third assumption from the gumption—Nature evolves *virtually* forever. Cosmic and thus Natural Evolution has gone on for billions and billions of years, and will continue on for billions and billions years more. Therefore, the sweet little poetic story of a 6-Day Creation 6,000 years ago is only a literary fable, at best...so say the Scientists, whose scientific progenitors *believed* that Story in the Stars. But, don't forget, *former* Scientific Believers...we can date Mazzaroth in his seasons to about 4000 BC, using nothing but those stars in the sky (see p. 46 ¶last)—just about 6000 years ago. And further, *former* Scientific Believers, let us not forget the I and II Laws of Thermodynamics.

I Law. Mass-energy is neither being created nor destroyed.

> **Gen 2:1 -3 Thus the heavens and the earth were finished, and all the host of them.** 2 And on the seventh day God **ended his work which he had made**; and he rested on the seventh day **from all his work which he had made**. 3 And God blessed the seventh day, and sanctified it: because that in it he had **rested from all his work which God created and made**.

II Law. All mass-energy is tending to entropy.

> **Heb 1:10-12 And, Thou, Lord, in the beginning hast laid the foundation of the earth; and the heavens are the works of thine hands: 11 They shall per-**

ish; but thou remainest; and **they all shall wax old as doth a garment**; 12 And **as a vesture shalt thou fold them up, and they shall be changed**: but thou art the same, and thy years shall not fail.

The Second Law says, in essence, everything is winding down. That logically and necessarily *implies* that everything used to be wound up. And that is exactly what the First Law *says*, in essence. Einstein and others assure us that the I and II Laws of Thermodynamics are the truest science that we have. Those Two Laws agree, in essence, with the Scriptural account of Creation. And internal evidence in both Mazzaroth and Scripture (see Appendix 1—The Bible Validated) give us a time frame for Creation of a little over 6000 years. Sadly, it would appear that *former* Believing Scientists have walked away from the Truth and given themselves over to Mathemagical Fables.

Ancient Scientists (primarily Astronomers) *believed* The Story in the Stars...*according to their own surviving clay tablet records*...for over 4000 years. They *believed* the Coming One would be born of a Virgin, battle The Serpent, be wounded unto death *upon a Cross*; then rise triumphant, having freed His Beloved Bride from The Serpent's coils, then leave promising to Come Again a Second Time. And then—Christ came...born of a Virgin, fulfilling in His lifetime all those prophetic aspects of the first two books of Mazzaroth, as well as 1500 Old Testament prophecies, including 300 of them *specifying His exact Identity...all without missing a single one*. Then, all the Scientists who had believed part or all of The Story in the Stars did an amazing thing.

They *rejected* Him...and just walked away, choosing to believe instead in Mathemagical Astrology Fairy Tales, first told in the clay tablets of Ancient Sumeria and Babylon.

The Jews, the Arabic Peoples, and the Scientists (primarily Astronomers, but some others)—all *believed* The Story in the Stars, and their ancient records prove it. Then, *when all the promises and the prophecies were fulfilled and proven True*—in the Person of The Lord Jesus Christ—most of them *rejected* Him...and just turned and walked away, leading most of the Human Race after them.

Amazing.

That Amazing Credibility Gap Thingy

Remember...a Credibility Gap is, An apparent difference between what is SAID or promised and WHAT HAPPENS OR IS TRUE. From the beginning of their historical records, the Jews, the Arabic Peoples, and the Scientists (primarily Astronomers, but some others) all SAID they believed Mazzaroth, and The Story in the Stars (and their ancient histories, in clay tablets and ancient writings, prove they did).

And THEN (2 BC-33 AD, 33 and 1/2 years...you have to remove 1 year, because there is no 0 AD), The Promised Seed of The Virgin, The Coming One, was born—He battled The Serpent for His Bride, was wounded unto death *upon a Cross*, yet rose from the dead, thus freeing His Bride from The Serpent's coils; then She watched in tears, as He was taken up to Heaven, promising Her that He would Come Again, crush The Serpent's head, and take Her home with Him...Forever. He not only fulfilled the detailed prophecies in the *first two* Books of Mazzaroth, but also 1500 Old Testament prophecies, including 300 of them *specifying His exact Identity...all without missing a single one.*

What was SAID in the first two Books of The Story in the Stars, and all those prophecies, ACTUALLY HAPPENED AND IS THEREFORE TRUE. And what was SAID was believed by the Jews, the Arabic Peoples, and the Scientists...UNTIL IT ACTUALLY HAPPENED AND WAS THEREFORE TRUE. Then, most of the Jews, most of the Arabic Peoples, and most of the Scientists, along with most of the Human Race *rejected* what ACTUALLY HAPPENED AND IS THEREFORE TRUE.

Isn't that amazing?

But...What about the *Third* Book of The Story in the Stars? The part of The Story that SAYS that The Bridegroom will COME AGAIN, to crush The Serpent's head and to Take His Bride Home. Will THAT actually happen and be proven true...*likewise*? Most of the Jews, most of the Arabic Peoples, most of the Scientists, along with most of the Human Race *do not* believe that.

There are *Two People*, however, who most definitely *do believe* The Bridegroom will Come Again:
THE SERPENT *and* THE BRIDE.

What do YOU believe?

> 2 Pet 3:3-7 Knowing this first, that **there shall come in the last days SCOFFERS**, walking after their own lusts, 4 And **saying, Where is the promise of his coming?** <u>for since the fathers fell asleep, all things continue as they were from the beginning of the creation.</u>
> <u>5 For this they willingly are ignorant of, that</u> **BY THE WORD OF GOD THE HEAVENS WERE OF OLD**, and the earth standing out of the water and in the water: 6 Whereby <u>the</u>

world that then was, being overflowed with water, perished: 7 **But the heavens and the earth, which are now, by the same word are kept in store, <u>reserved unto fire</u> against THE DAY OF JUDGMENT and perdition of ungodly men**.

As I told you in the beginning (p. 4),

> GOD *is the Author of all True Religion,*
> SATAN *is the Author of all False Religion, and*
> EACH *False Religion persecutes ALL other religions—*
> THAT *is just the way it is.*

AND SO IT WAS...

...That in the manner outlined herein, The Story in the Stars was told for over 2000 years. Then...God called the Patriarch Abram out of Ur of the Chaldees, changed his name to Abraham (Father of Many Nations, Gen 17:5), and began to tighten the Bloodline into a road made ready for The Coming One, leading to a Jewish Virgin's Womb...2000 more years later. Then...HE Came...And **HE DID IT!**

And NOW, again 2000 more years later, The Jews have Returned to The Land (1948), and their nation was born in a day (14 May 1948, Isa 66:7-8), and the Times of the Gentiles are over (Luke 21:20-24). NOW, we are waiting in these Last Days, in this Last Generation (Mtt 24:34; Mk 13:30; Lk 21:32)—we are waiting for THE BRIDEGROOM WHO IS COMING THAT SECOND TIME, to Come and to smash the Serpent's Head...and Forever Embrace His Bride:

> Rev 21:2,9-10,27 And I John saw **the holy city, new Jerusalem**, coming down from God out of heaven, <u>**prepared as a BRIDE adorned for her HUSBAND**</u>....9 And there came unto me one of the seven angels which had the seven vials full of the seven last plagues, and talked with me, saying, **Come hither, I will show thee** THE BRIDE, THE LAMB'S WIFE. 10 And he carried me away in the spirit to a great and high mountain, and showed me **that great city, the holy Jerusalem**, descending out of heaven from God, ...27 And there shall in no wise enter into it any thing that defileth, neither whatsoever worketh abomination, or maketh a lie: but <u>THEY **which are written in the** LAMB'**s book of life**</u>.

And so ENDS The Story in The Stars...

Told by Mazzaroth in His Season, to the Patriarchs...and then Told by the Old Testament, to the Jews...and then Told by the New Testament, to the Church...and now Told by the Church, to the World—for, you see, they are all ONE AND THE SAME STORY:

The Bridegroom, dual-natured Seed of the Woman, Coming to Defeat the Serpent and be wounded terribly unto Death, but to Rise victorious; then to Leave and Come Again, and Destroy the Serpent, and Gather His Bride, the Woman's Other Seed, and take Her Home...FOREVER.

Rev 22:20 ...Even so, Come, Lord Jesus.

*****

Glossary

Brainwashing. Make (someone) adopt radically different beliefs by using systematic and often forcible pressure: *the organization could brainwash young people | they have been brainwashed into conformity and subservience.* [Oxford American]

> The "systematic and often forcible pressure" is thoroughly defined by *Cognitive Dissonance* (see Wikipedia article). The "radically different beliefs" are adequately defined by *Normalcy Bias* (see Wikipedia article). In other words, victims are *cognitively dissonated* (so to speak) until they adopt the desired *normalcy bias*. In a larger context, *Brainwashing* is a subset of Propaganda. It's what they do to your head at Harvard and other fine universities, if you stay there too long (again, so to speak).
>
>> **propaganda.** *chiefly derogatory* information, especially of a biased or misleading nature, used to promote or publicize a particular political cause or point of view.
>> • the dissemination of propaganda as a political strategy: *the party's leaders believed that a long period of education and propaganda would be necessary.* [Oxford American]
>
> In the Marine Corps, I was trained in the basics of resisting *Brainwashing*. There are 3 steps.
>
>> *Define*—What your belief system is, and what the "radically different system" being forced is.
>>
>> *Contrast*—the major points of each, in black and white terms, so there is no doubt.
>>
>> *Ridicule*—every differing point in the "radically different system", relentlessly, and laugh and laugh and laugh ... because...what you can *prove* is absurd can never bind your mind.
>
> *Define, Contrast, Ridicule* (DCR)—This is the *only* Door Out, from the prison of Propaganda. Every rational mind has a choice: *Submit* on your knees, or choose to run *Free*. This—DCR—is that Door.

Dum-dum Doo-doo. We will study each component of this highly technical term separately, then clarify the combination.

> **dum-dum.** A <u>stupid</u> person. Origin 1970s: reduplication of dumb. [Oxford American]

stupid. Lacking intelligence or common sense: *I was stupid enough to think she was perfect.*
- dazed and unable to think clearly: *apprehension was numbing her brain and making her stupid.* [Oxford American]

doo-doo. A child's word for excrement, used euphemistically in other contexts: *when our fax machine isn't working, we're in deep doo-doo.* [Oxford American]

excrement. Waste matter discharged from the bowels; feces. [Oxford American]

Etymological Note. *Dum-dum* essentially means stupid, so mental productive flow is the concept here; likewise, *stupid* includes the conceptual *lack* of logical coherence. And of course, *Doo-doo* is essentially waste matter even a rectum no longer wants to retain, just lumpy stinky stuff whose sole existential purpose is, apparently, to make a nose gag. Thus, we can quite accurately *conceive* of Dum-dum Doo-doo as *doo-doo* mentally produced by a *dum-dum*. Now, we are ready to formulate the *technical* term.

Dum-dum doo-doo (technical term). Noun. Any mental production expressible (or not) in words and/or mathematics, in any sort of way, which is effectively illogical or demonstrably reducible to sophistry, and which is linguistically excreted in any manner whatsoever (or not) by a person so functionally stupid and/or so functionally brainless and/or so functionally foolish (for whatever reason) as to qualify as a dum-dum: *What kind of twit dreamed up this pile of dum-dum doo-doo?*

May be used metaphorically, under conditions of robust resemblance: *Believe it or not, this dum-dum doo-doo got him a Nobel Peace Prize.*

Final Note. <u>Always</u> use this technical term <u>precisely</u>, lest people think you are being crude.

Mathemagic. A system of mathematical sophistry involving, but not limited to, equating *True* with mathematical *Validity*—The deception of misleading people with mathematical equations and models, by declaring that such mathematics offered as proof of an Assertion (to make it *Plausibly Credible*), *if it is mathematically Valid*, must also be *True* in the world of real actual things.

[I invented the word (as far as I know), so I can guarantee this definition. COJ]

Engineers argue about this with contrary theoreticians all the time. Any mathematics that seeks to *truthfully* describe the real world of actual objects and forces, *must continually* relate, adjust, and re-relate to those actual objects and forces, *in order to truthfully describe the way things actually are.* The moment one divorces one's mathematics from *rigid continuous correlation with real world things*, that moment one mentally steps away into La-La Land, a world of pure fantasy, where there can exist parallel universes, where universes can Big-Bang into existence out of nothing, where live things can evolve from dead things, where *Anything* conceivable is believable...if only you accept the mathematical *Validity* of a model as being the same as *True*.

Mathematically *Valid* is only correct grammar for equations, just as correct grammar with words produces correct sentences—but, grammatically correct sentences, just as mathematically valid equations, can be quite *Untrue*, and not at all the way real things actually are. All the best fairy tales are grammatically correct. That's why I call it Mathe-*magic*—a theoretician, from a fine school like Harvard, can thus simply wave his *valid* mathemagic model, and make a gob of dum-dum doo-doo (technical meaning only) **P**iled **h**igh and **D**eep look...*sooo Reeaal*...and smell *sooo sweeeet*.

*****

Appendix 1—The Bible Validated

Proof that Only One God Exists

There are two...and only two...kinds of people: Those who are Born Again, and believe God exists, and Those who are Born Against, and do not. Even if one tries to imagine a third kind of person, a Doubter, it comes back to the fact there are only the same two kinds of those: Those that doubt that God is, and those that doubt that God isn't.

From a certain point of view, it is impossible to prove the existence of God to a Believer, precisely because *they know it already without the evidence!* They are literally, by the ineffable grace of God, born again to believe. For a similar reason, it is impossible to prove the existence of God to an Infidel, precisely because *they refuse to believe despite the evidence!* They are literally, by the terrible tragedy of Sin, born against any possibility of belief. Strictly speaking, you can *convince* (to make somebody sure or certain of something) a Believer; and you can *argue* (to give reasons for an opinion in order to support it) with an Infidel; but, you can't actually *prove* it to either.

So, why discuss it? For two good reasons. First, to confirm the faith of the Believer (and also to confirm the suspicions of someone who doubts that God isn't). Second, to shut the mouth of the Infidel (and also that of someone who doubts that God is). The fact is that proof remains proof even if nobody believes it; and unproven remains unproven even if everybody believes it. You see, it does not matter doodly-squat what anybody *believes*—what is, *IS*; and what ain't, *AIN'T*. That's just the way it is.

So, let's look first at *Possibilities*.

Curiously, there are *only two Possibilities*: Either, There is a God (Theism); or, There is no God (Atheism). *Intriguingly*, these two possibilities are, logically speaking, necessary contraries—If either is false, the other must be true. *Fascinatingly*, the proposition "There is no God" is a universal negative and *cannot* be proven. That *necessarily* leaves only one other possibility...There is a God. Necessary contraries, you see—If either is false, the other *must* be true.

Next, let's consider *Probability*. Blaise Pascal (1623–62) was a French mathematician, physicist, and religious philosopher. He founded the theory of probabilities, which we are going to find immensely useful in a moment. Pascal was a Theist. He argued the *probability* of God's existence in what became known as Pascal's Wager. I *adapted* this version, from a reference source.

Pascal's Wager

If God does not exist, then an Atheist and a Theist have the same fate: Nothing.

- *Thus there is <u>no</u> eternal advantage to being correct in Atheism.* In addition, there is no temporal advantage either, since Atheists do not seem to be happier than Theists, in fact they seem much less so in most cases.
- Also, the Atheist can never know he was correct, and the Theist can never know he was wrong.

If God does exist, then an Atheist will likely suffer eternally for rejecting belief in God; at least his Atheism will not help him. The Theist, however, will likely live in eternal happiness with God; at least his Theism will not hurt him.

- *Thus there <u>is</u> an eternal advantage in being correct in Theism.*
- Also, the Theist will know forever his is correct, and the Atheist will always know and regret that he was wrong.

Therefore, it is *more reasonable* to believe in God.

How about that? It is *possible* to prove that God exists (and *impossible* to prove that He doesn't), and it is also *probable* that God exists. That raises another Question: Is it possible that *more than one* God can exist, and if so, how probable is that? Short Answer: Nope, and Squat.

The Long Answer is the proof of the unicity of God. Unicity is a word the philosophers use to emphasize the *absolute oneness* of god. Unicity means: If there is a god, then there is only one—there is not, nor can be, another. I have borrowed and modified this proof from Dulles, Demske, and O'Connell, *Introductory Metaphysics* (Sheed and Ward, 1955; Question 15, pp. 192-196). It goes like this:

Proof of the Unicity of God

Major premise—Two or more Infinite Beings could conceivably differ from one another either by actuality or by potentiality.

Proof—These are the only two possibilities.

Minor premise—But, neither of these two alternatives is possible.

Proof—Whether actually or potentially, this difference must be either

- a) the sum total of existential perfection which they did or could possess, in which case they would be both alike and different for the same reason, which is contradictory and absurd; or
- b) some perfection *added to* the sum total of existential perfection which they did or could possess, in which case they both would be finite and not infinite.

Conclusion—Therefore, there can be only one Infinite Being.

Proof—Since the major premise stated the only two conceivable ways there could be more than one god, and since both were shown to be impossible, there can only be one God.

So...where are we, up to now? We have found that it is *possible* to prove there is a God (and *impossible* to prove there isn't), also *probable* that there is one, and *certain* (if so) that there can be only one God. Now, let us consider a proof for the existence of God.

Since this proof deals with Prophecy, I recommend the resource text, *Encyclopedia of Biblical Prophecy*, by J. Barton Payne (Baker Book House, 1973, 7th printing 1989; 754 pp). This proof is *so* good, I just stole it from God:

The Proof from Prophecy (The Foreteller)

Isa 46:9-11 **Remember the former things of old: for I AM GOD, AND THERE IS NONE ELSE; I AM GOD, AND THERE IS NONE LIKE ME, 10 <u>Declaring the end from the beginning, and from ancient times the things that are not yet done,</u>** saying, My counsel shall stand, and I will do all my pleasure: 11 Calling a ravenous bird from the east, the man that executeth my counsel from a far country: **yea, I have spoken it, I will also bring it to pass; I have purposed it, I will also do it.**

There are 1800 Prophecies in The Bible— 1500 fulfilled, and 300 yet future:

1189 chap	1.5 Prophecies per Chap, or 3 per 2 Chap
31,173 vss	1 Prophecy per 17.3 verses
773,692 words	1 Prophecy per 430 words

Some of the OT prophecies stretch over hundreds, even thousands of years, such as The Seed of The Woman, which spanned 4 thousand years. All of the 300 unfulfilled prophecies have now reached over 1900 years, some well over 2000 years, and a few like The Battle of Armageddon nearly 3000 years. *Yet, there is not one single missed prophecy.*

WHAT ARE THE ODDS those 1500 fulfilled prophecies, without a single miss, were fulfilled by chance (i.e., not Purposefully)? Use the simplest possible odds, 50-50 for each: **1 in $1/0.5^{1500}$**. How big is that number? One estimate (wordiq.com/definition/Electron) is there are at least 10^{79} electrons in the known universe, and that 10^{130} could be crammed in belly button to backbone like a bowl of grits. A wad of 0.5^{1500} electrons so jammed together would require 10^{1370} universes to hold them...that's several gazillion, trust me. Mark one electron with an "X", toss it back, then stir the pile. Close your eyes and pick one electron. The chance you'll pick the one with the "X" is the chance all those prophecies happened by chance. *All those other electrons* are the *probability* that those prophecies *were done on Purpose*.

Another way to look at it. Mathematicians tell us that the limits of mathematical meaningfulness, when dealing with guesstimates, are $n \times 10^{\pm 50}$. 0.5^{1500} is 0.5^{1450} orders of magnitude *larger* than the limits of mathematical meaningfulness. In other words, a guesstimate that huge does not mean squat...*it could not happen by chance, only by Purpose.* Conclusion—Those 1500 prophecies, without a single miss, did not happen by chance, *they were brought to pass on Purpose.*

What is the chance that the 300 remaining prophecies will be fulfilled? Why, no *chance* at all—those 300 prophecies will be brought to pass by the same *Absolute Purpose* we *now know* fulfilled the other 1500 prophecies, without a single miss. Since the Return of Israel to the Land, and their hegemony over Jerusalem, those fulfillments have started happening already.

WHAT KIND OF FORETELLER does that require? Such a Foreteller must be:

Omniscient	To *know* all possible details of the encompassed events
Omnipotent	To *guarantee* all possible details of the encompassed events
Omnipresent	To *supervise* all possible details of the encompassed events

Consider. Each prophecy of Absolute Purpose, *upon fulfillment*, became a statement of Absolute Truth. Therefore, 1500 such fulfilled prophecies constitute Absolute Validation of the Absolute Truthfulness of such a Foreteller (because the fulfillments were due, not to chance, but to Absolute Purpose). But, that Foreteller *also* prophesies of the End of this universe and the Beginning of another.

Such an Absolutely Truthful Foreteller, that can fulfill such prophecies as those, logically must be:

    Eternal   To comprehend the End of this universe and the Beginning of another

    Infinite   To comprehend the Fullness of two consecutive yet different Universes

CONCLUSION—Such a Foreteller...being Omniscient, Omnipotent, Omnipresent, Eternal, and Infinite...by definition *must* be God.

The Bible Validated

We have proven the Absolute Truthfulness of the Foreteller (based upon the same odds that proved Purpose, since each fulfilled prophecy is thus necessarily a statement of Absolute Truth). *The Foreteller claims to have inspired all of The Holy Bible, which claim must be True, given the Absolute Truthfulness of the Foreteller.* Therefore, every statement in The Holy Bible must necessarily be True, since all are, in effect, statements made by an Absolutely Truthful Foreteller...therefore,

> *1500 FULFILLED PROPHECIES WITHOUT A SINGLE MISS VALIDATE EVERY STATEMENT IN THE HOLY BIBLE.*

Thus, The Holy Bible is not only True, but may be confidently cited as a source of Truth, which is an accurate representation of Reality (which, of course, is The Way Things Actually Are).

ONLY THE HOLY BIBLE—of all the books, holy scriptures, and literature of Mankind—has this kind of incredible prophetic structure and this kind of *scientific* validation (i.e., Archaeology and positive Mathematical Probability). *It is estimated that over 25% of Scripture is either telling, fulfilling, or discussing these prophecies.* They are inextricably embedded, together with their Truthfulness, in the warp and woof of Scripture—in every 20.8 verses of Scripture (on average), there is a *fulfilled* prophesy using over 5 of those verses. **To ignore this kind of validating evidence**—together with this overwhelming degree of archaeological confirmation and favorable mathematical probability—**is the response of an utter ass.**

For additional complete, thorough, logical, and scientific arguments for the existence of God, see my monograph, **Does God *Really* Exist?** (go internet to "lulu.com", then choose *Shop*, then type *Conrad Jarrell*; also on Amazon).

*****

Appendix 2—
The Constellations Illustrated

THE STORY IN THE STARS
Pictures of the Constellations

Always remember, The Story in The Stars is found in the NAMES of the constellations and their brightest stars, NOT in the pictures. The pictures are only aids to *visualizing* the star groupings, and tend to vary greatly between regions and times. *Always* check the Descriptions and Definitions of each constellation, to best form that *mental* picture. The pictures are ordered into 3 Books, exactly as was the *verbal* explanation of Mazzaroth.

I have copied these pictures from those in Seiss's book, but re-sized them as needed, to fit them on these pages. Therefore, the printing in each may be greatly reduced (so you might have to look closely and squint). Since the key information is given in the fully worded section anyway, I'm only using these pictures to sketch an outline around the constellations.

Also, if you look closely around the edges of the pictures, you will see bits of the surrounding constellations identified, which helps you to relate each one to the surrounding constellations of the Zodiac.

THE FIRST BOOK—
THE REDEEMER, <u>HIS 1ST COMING</u>

1. VIRGO—THE PROMISED SEED OF THE WOMAN

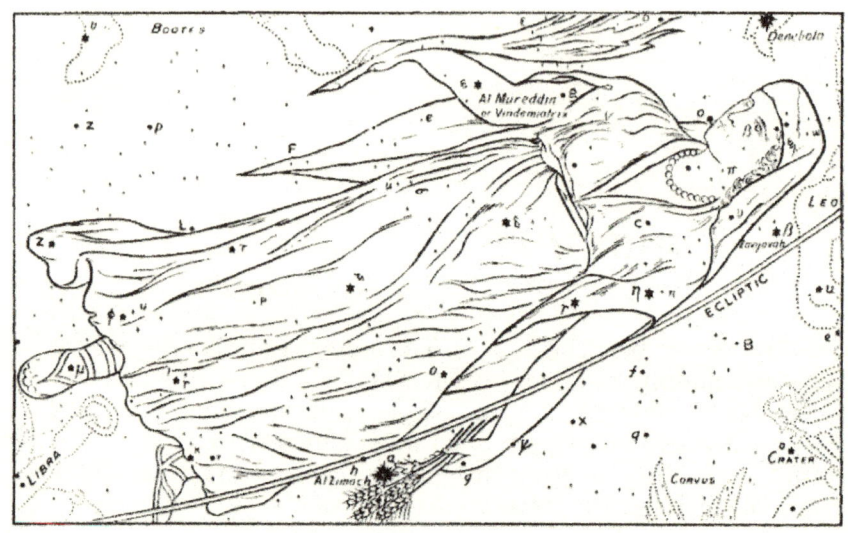

COMA—The Desire of all nations.

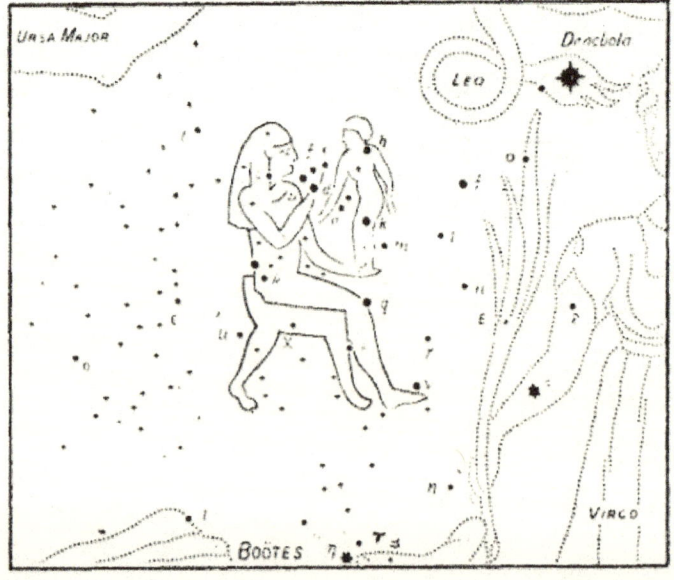

CENTAURUS—The Despised Sin-offering.

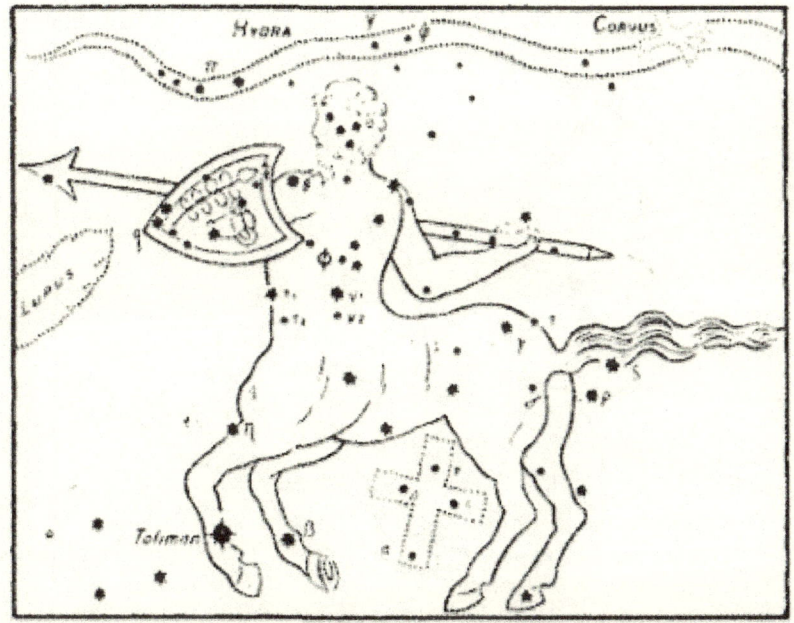

BOÖTES—The Coming Judge.

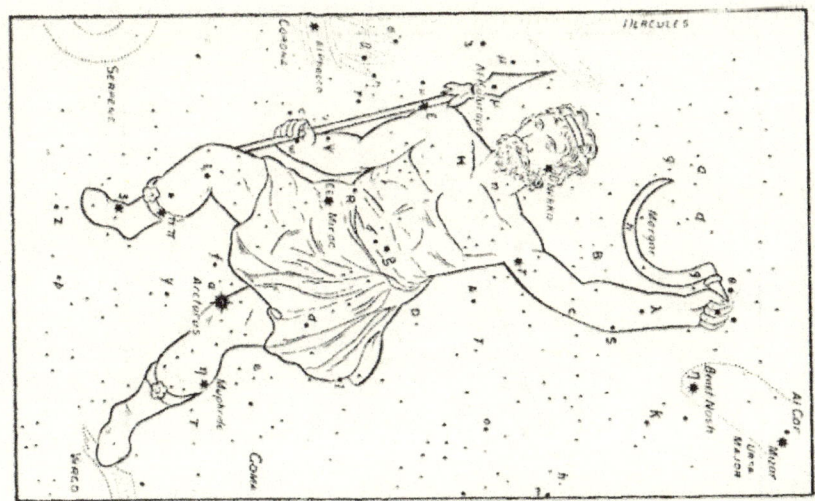

2. LIBRA—The Scales, The Redeemer's Atoning Work.

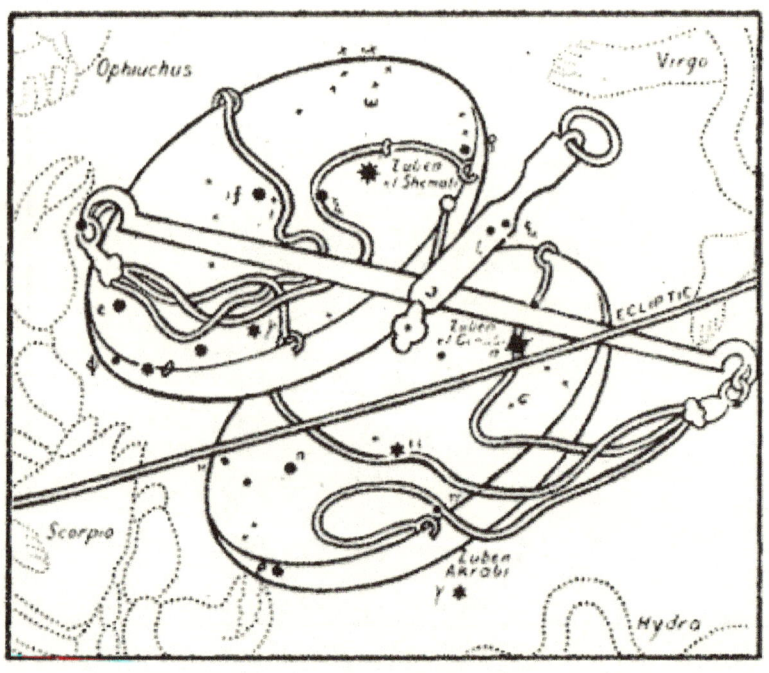

Crux—The Southern Cross.

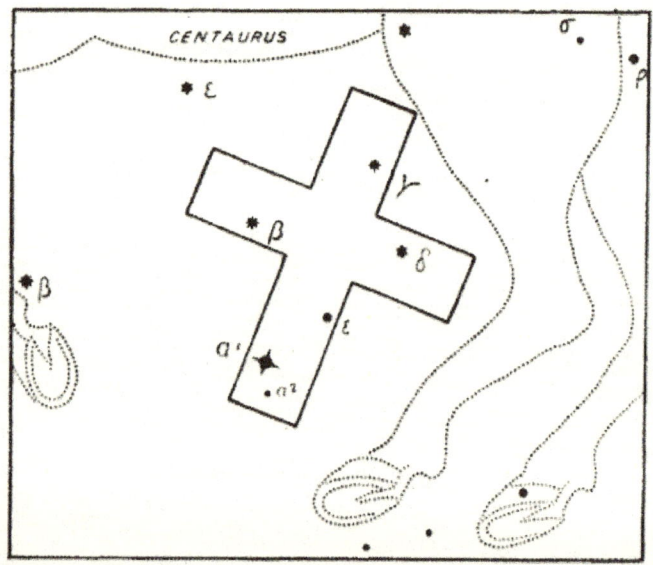

Victima—The Slain Victim.

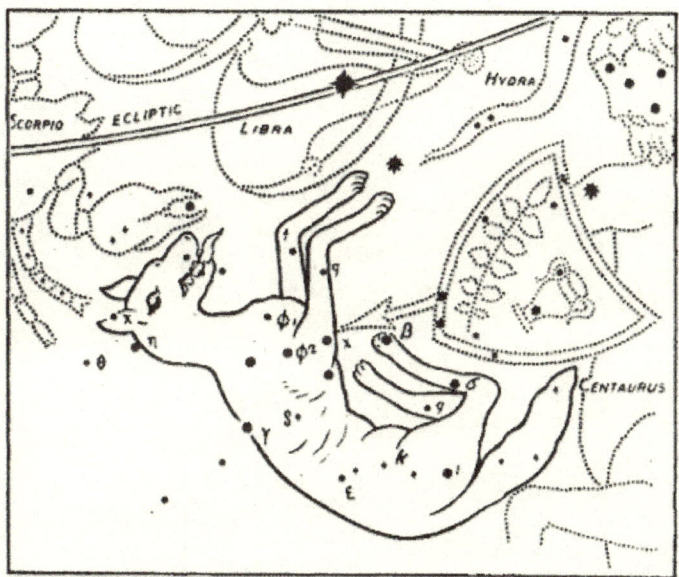

Corona—The Northern Crown.

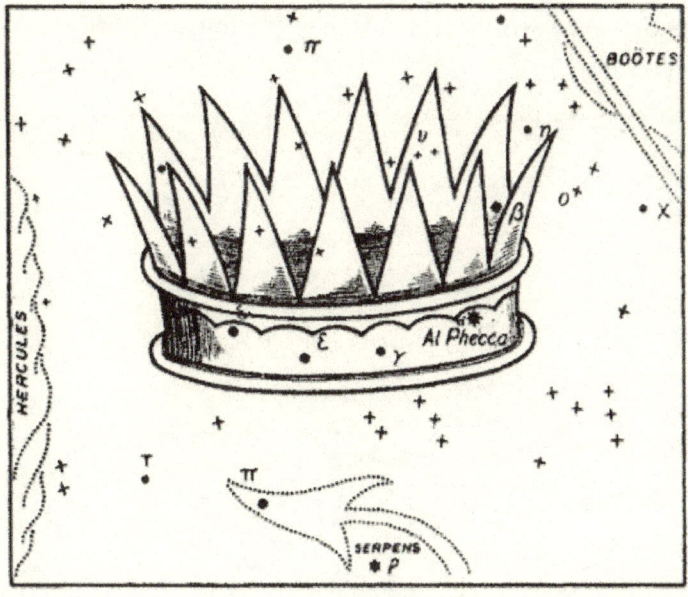

3. **SCORPIO**—The Redeemer's Conflict.

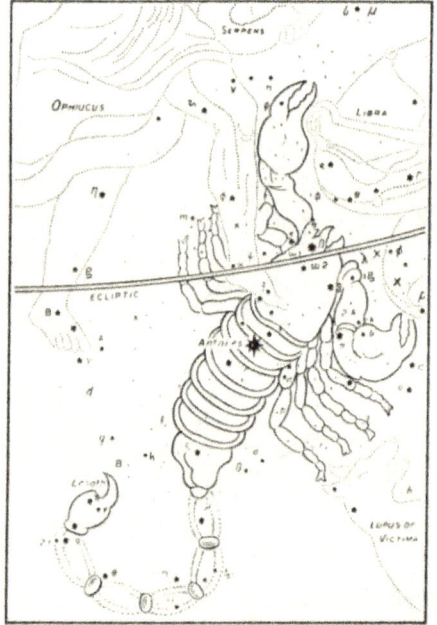

OPHIUCUS SERPENS—A Powerful Man struggling with a Serpent.

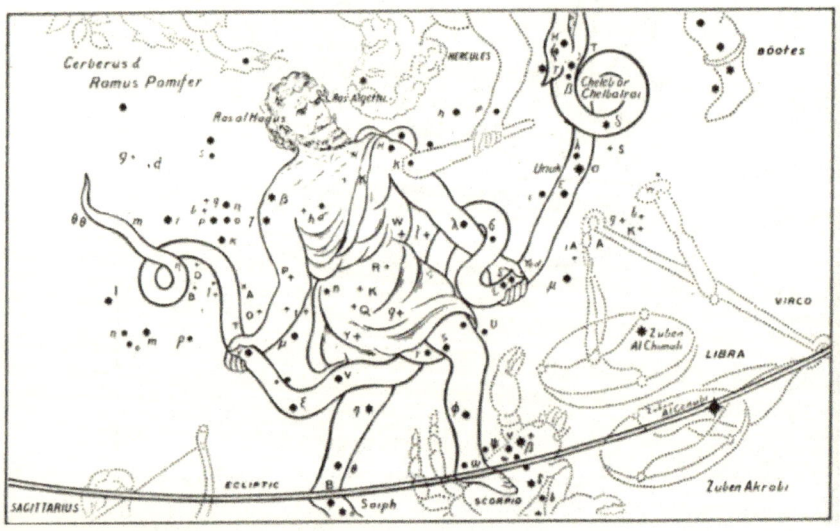

HERCULES— A mighty man kneeling, contending with a Monster.

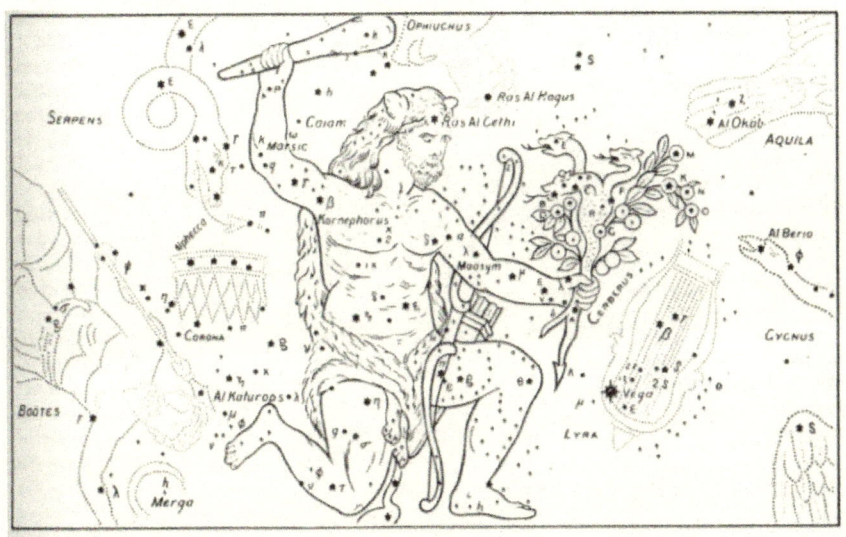

4. SAGITTARIUS—THE CENTAUR BATTLING THE SCORPION

LYRA—The Harp

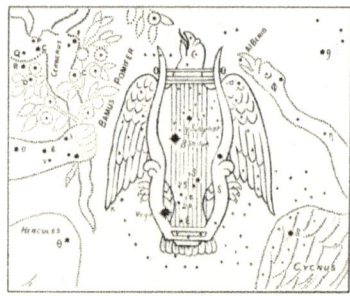

ARA—A Burning Altar

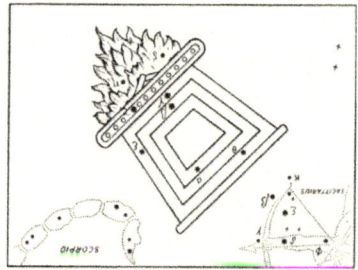

DRACO—A Great Coiled Dragon

THE SECOND BOOK—
THE REDEEMED, BLESSINGS PROCURED

5. CAPRICORNUS—A HALF-GOAT WITH A FISH'S TAIL.

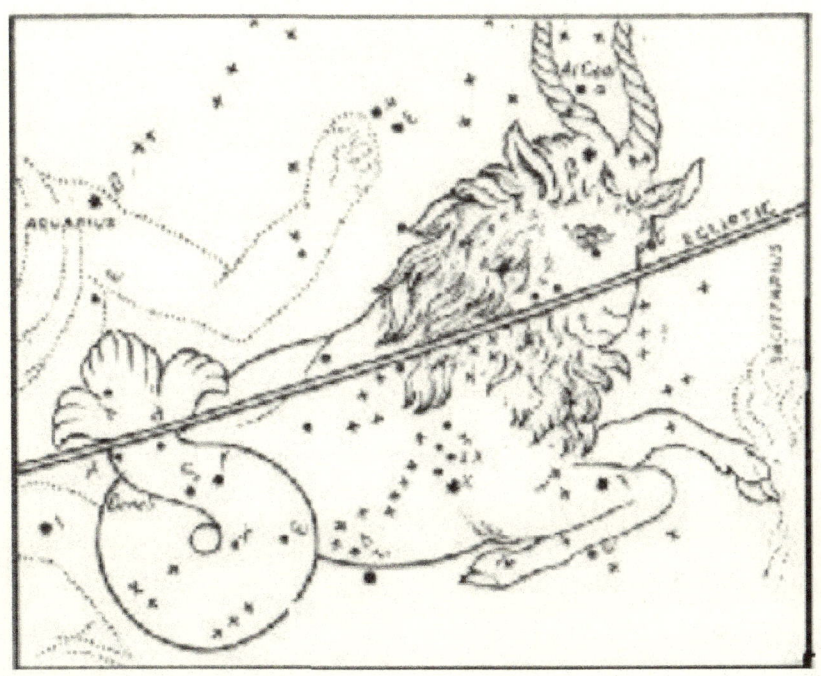

SAGITTA—An Arrow.

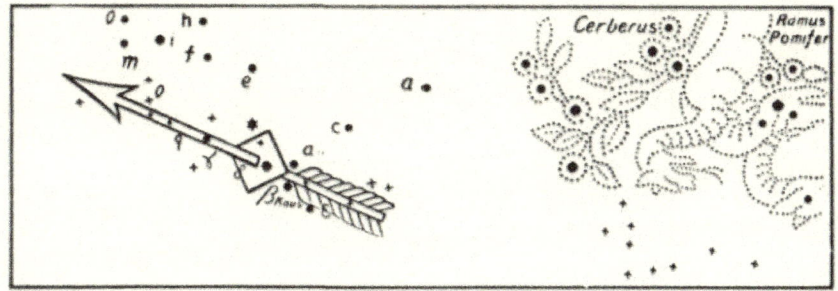

AQUILA—A falling Eagle.

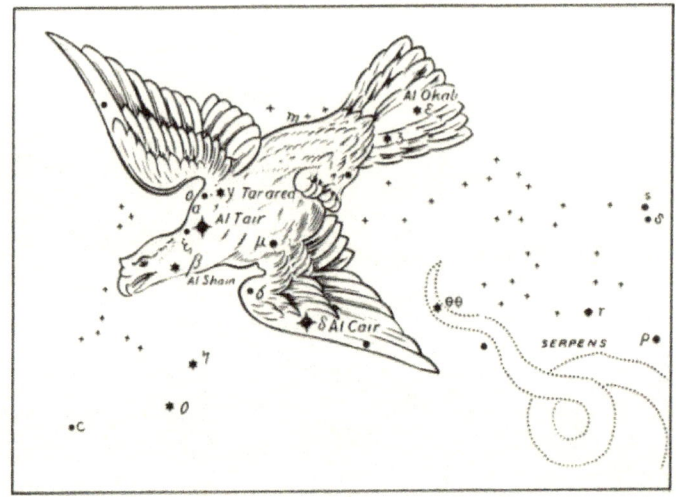

DELPHINUS—A leaping Fish.

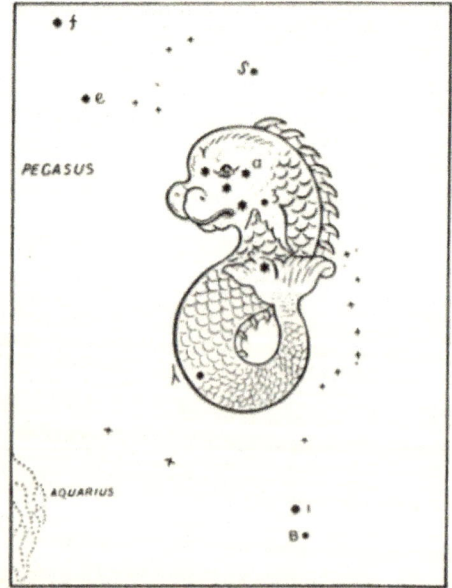

6. AQUARIUS—A MAN POURING WATER FROM AN URN

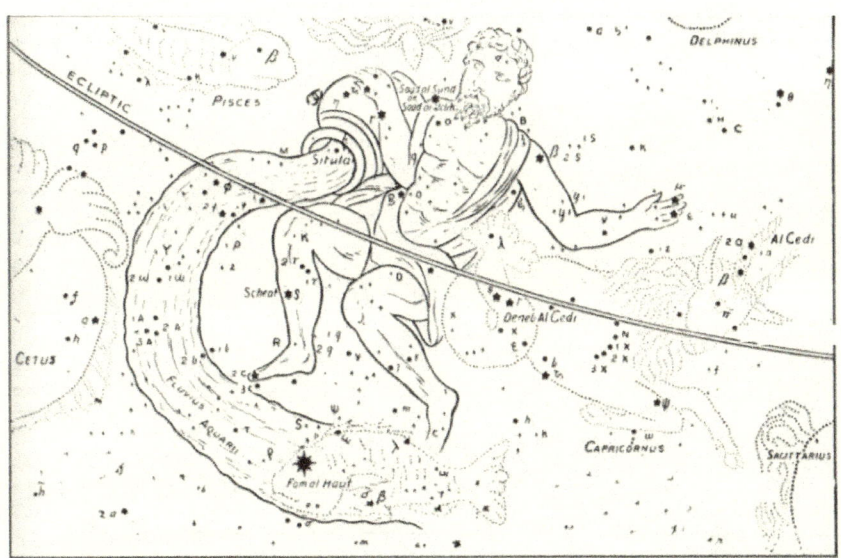

PISCIS AUSTRALIS—A large Fish.

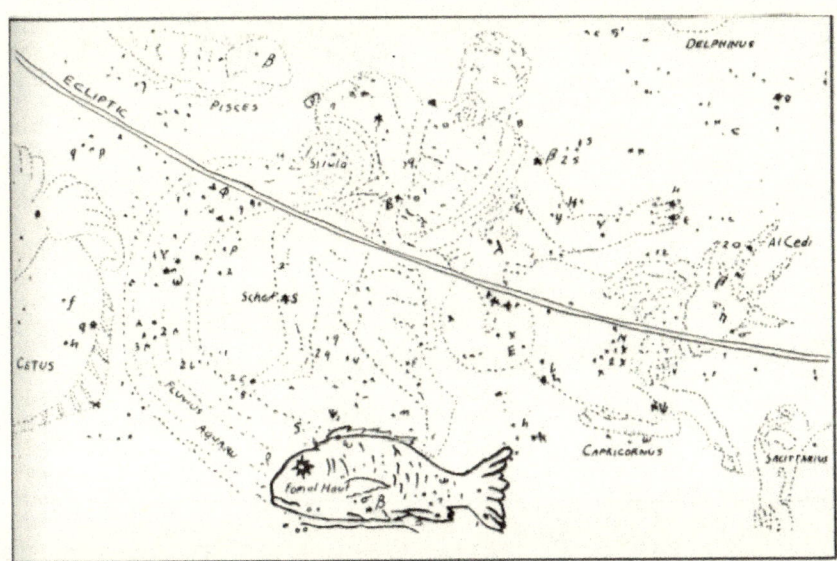

PEGASUS—A winged Horse.

CYGNUS—A great Swan.

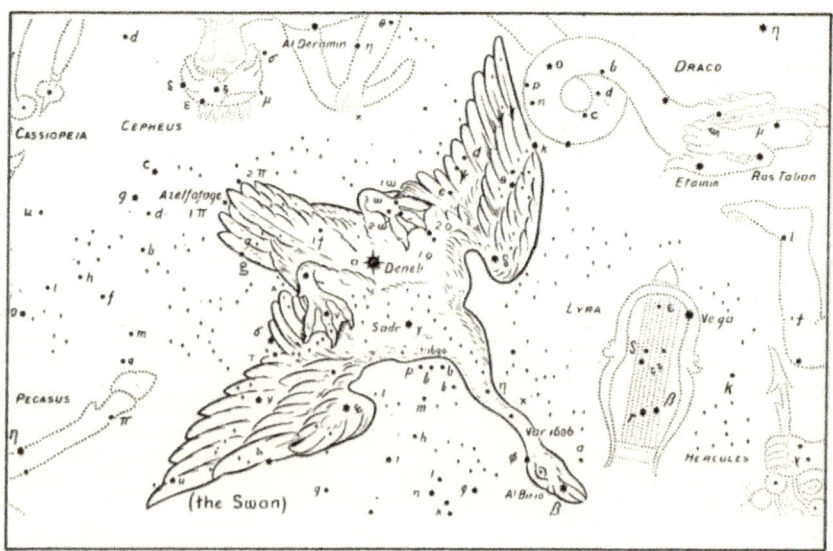

7. PISCES—TWO LARGE FISHES BOUND TOGETHER

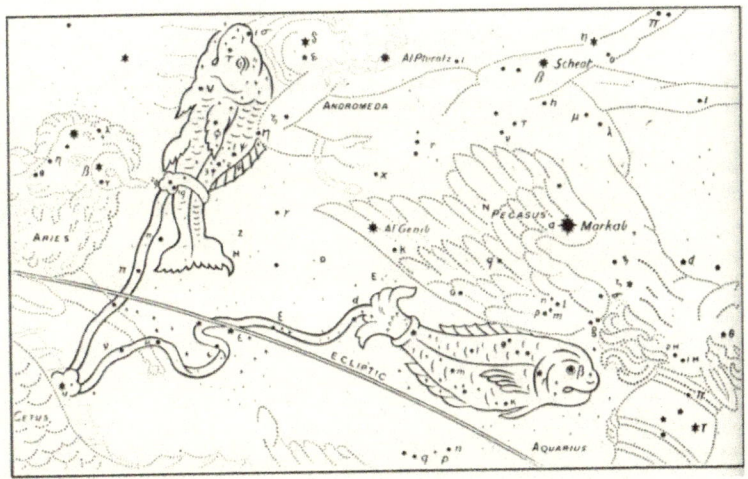

ANDROMEDA—A helpless Woman, bound by chains.

CEPHEUS—A King, seated in glory.

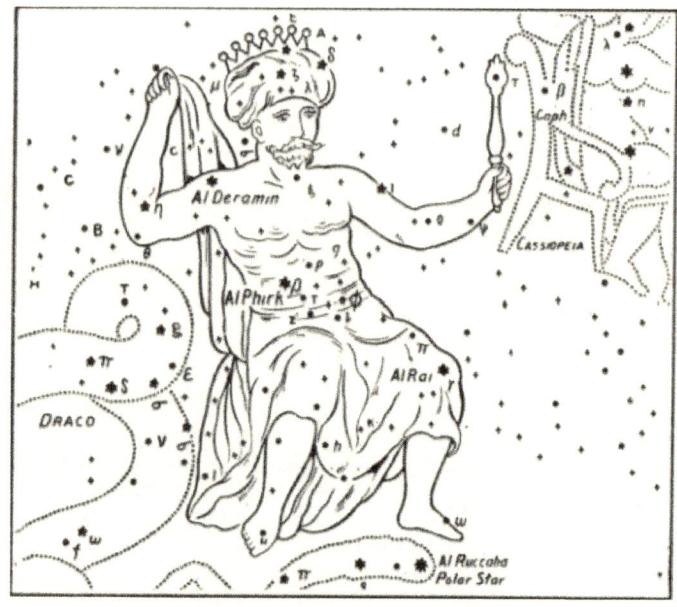

8. ARIES—THE RAM, BLESSINGS CONSUMMATED

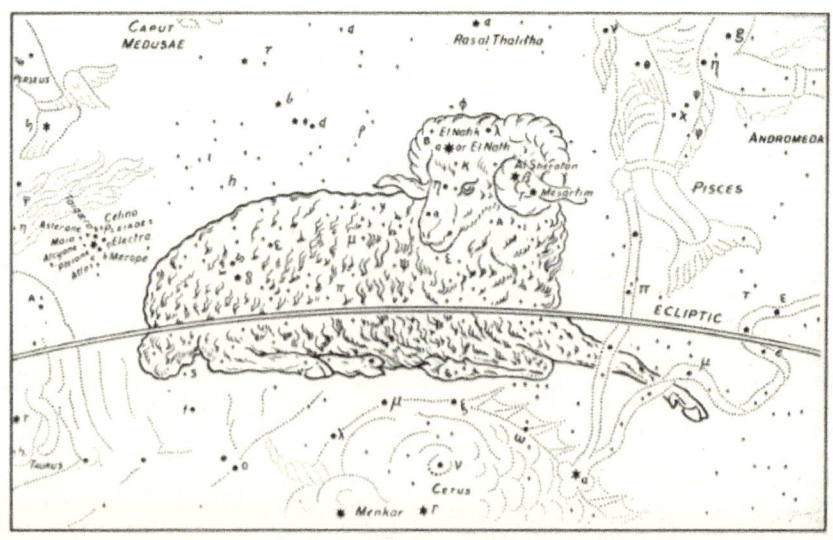

Cassiopeia—A Woman set free, enthroned beside a King.

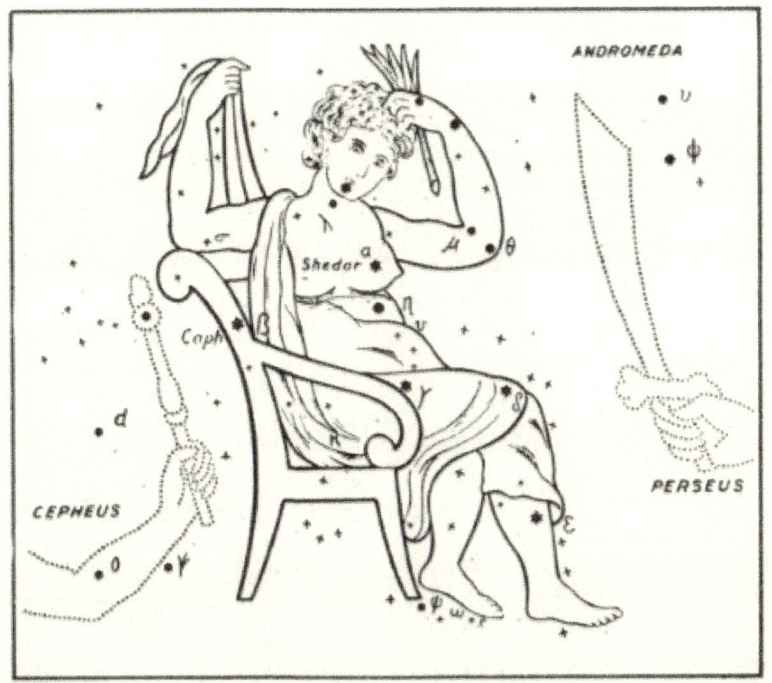

Cetus—The Sea Monster.

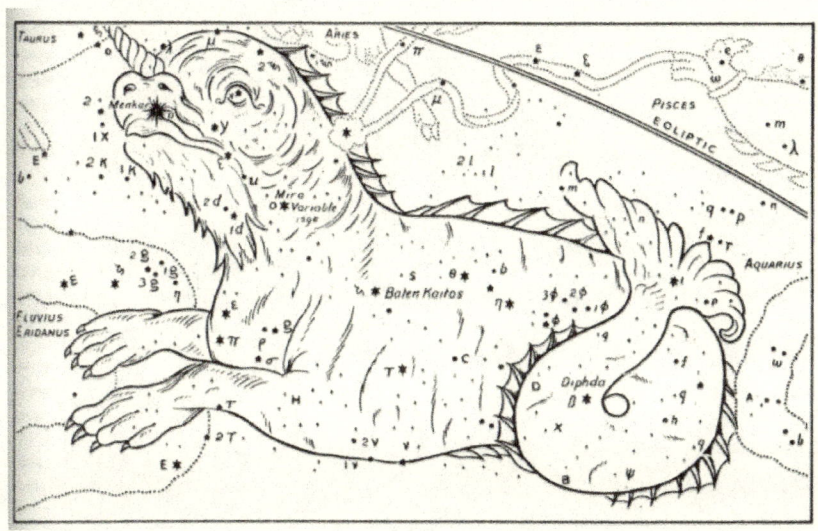

PERSEUS—Mighty Man with a sword and a severed head.

THE THIRD BOOK—
THE REDEEMER, HIS 2ND COMING

9. TAURUS—THE COMING JUDGE

ORION—A Mighty Hunter, with a club and severed Lion's head.

ERIDANUS—A great flowing River.

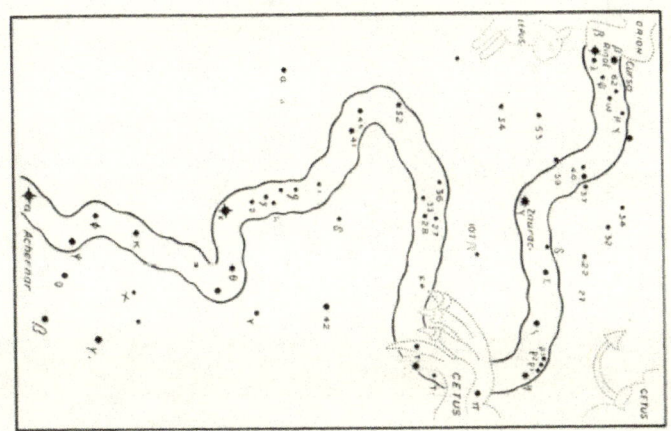

AURIGA—A seated Shepherd, holding a She-goat and Two Kids.

10. GEMINI—TWO-FOLD NATURE OF THE JUDGE

LEPUS—A large Hare.

CANIS MAJOR—A large Dog.

CANIS MINOR—A smaller Dog.

11. CANCER—THE REDEEMED POSSESSIONS

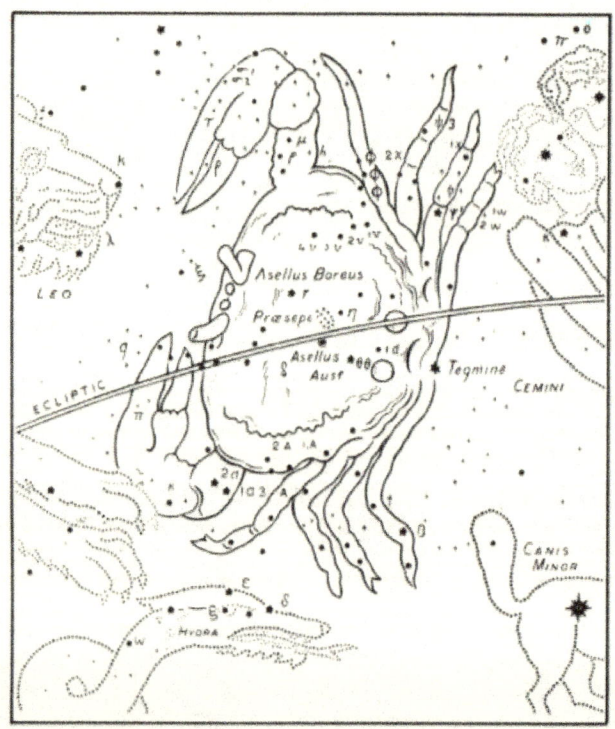

URSA MINOR—A small Bear.

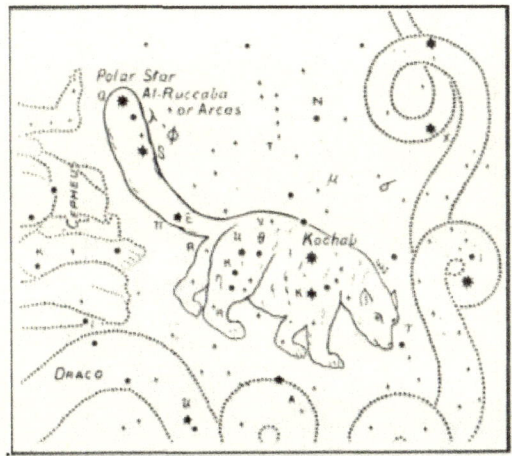

URSA MAJOR—A large Bear.

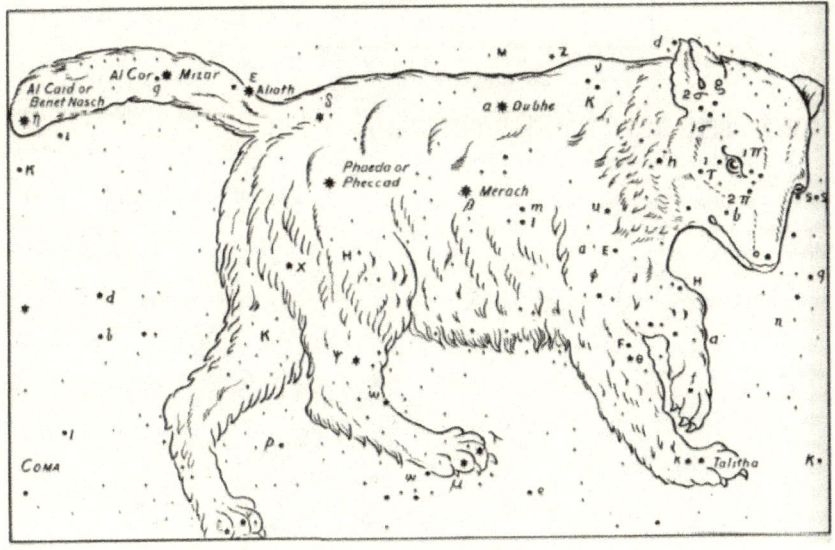

ARGO—A Ship.

12. LEO—THE REDEEMER'S TRIUMPH

HYDRA—A huge Serpent; **CRATER**—A Large Cup;
CORVUS—A Bird of Prey

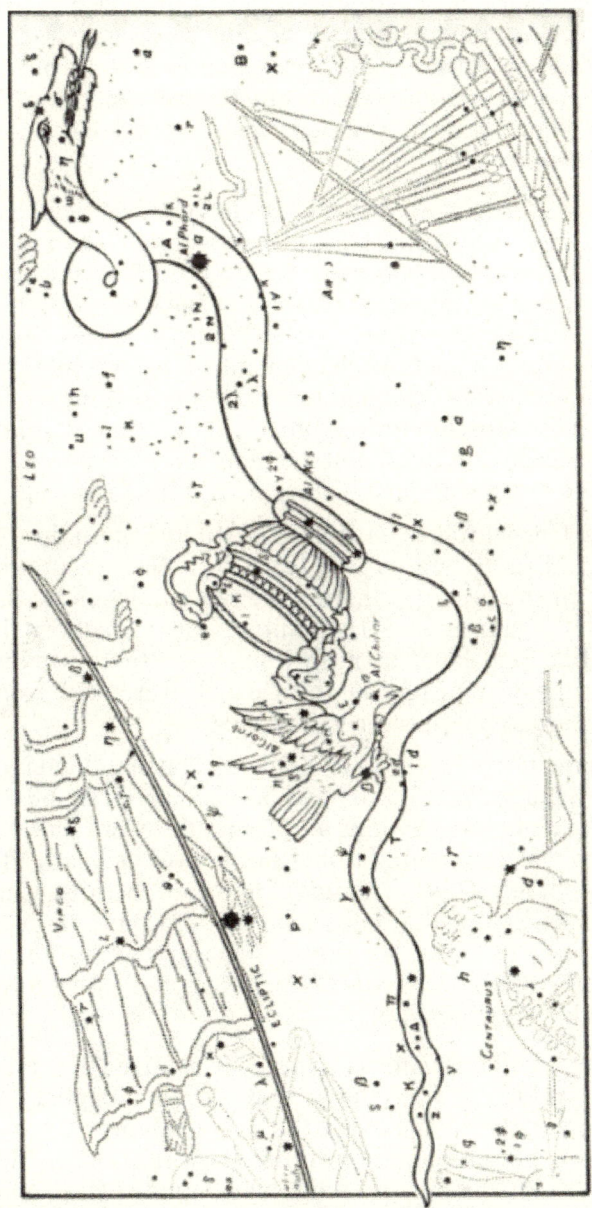

finis

About the Author

Elder Conrad Jarrell is a duly ordained minister of a Welsh-type Baptist Church. That means a *type* of Baptist Church whose organization is Independent, Congregational, 5-point Sovereign Grace (TULIP—similar to Presbyterians, only *much more* so) and which can be traced *directly* back through Welsh Baptist immigrants from England, many of whom came to America in the colonial days, some coming over as *entire congregations.*

In England, Welsh-type Baptist Churches can be traced back directly through their Anabaptist ("again-baptizers", as their opponents started calling them) predecessors in Wales, Cornwall, and parts of Britain, through the Middle Ages, all the way back to 130 AD, when the Anabaptists first planted churches in Wales. This was 195 years *before* the Roman Catholic Church came into existence in 325 AD, at the Council of Nicaea—*proclaimed into existence* by Emperor Constantine, at the time *an unbaptized pagan*. Please note that *no* infallible pope even existed at that point, let alone endorsed such *heathen* pomposity. J.R. Graves, Baptist historian, said the following:

> That the Gospel was extensively spread in Britain during this period [2nd century] we learn from Tertullian and Origen. In the year 130 there were two ministers by the names of Faganus and Damianus, who were born in Wales, but were born again in Rome, and there becoming imminent ministers of the Gospel, were sent from Rome to assist their brethren in Wales.

Those Anabaptist Churches around Rome had been ministered to by the Apostles Paul and Peter, both of whom died about 67-68 AD, a little over 60 years before Faganus and Damianus were sent to Wales. The apostles ministered around Rome a little over 30 years after The Last Supper in 33 AD. This is *crucially* important, because Christ the Pastor, administering the first Lord's Supper, or Communion, proves the fully functioning Church *incontestably existed at that time*—292 YEARS BEFORE the Roman Catholic Church was proclaimed into existence by an unbaptized heathen.

Why is that significant? Jesus Christ was baptized by a man He four times denominated "John the Baptist". When a Baptist preacher baptizes a believer, they come out of the water a Baptist. They do *not* come out a Methepiscoterianatholicampbellitormon. Jesus Christ was a Baptist, *exactly* like the preacher who baptized Him, and He founded a Baptist Church, which has *continually existed to this day*. Elder Conrad Jarrell is a duly ordained minister of THAT Church.

Made in the USA
Monee, IL
18 June 2020